THE · LISTENER'S · GUIDE · TO

Medieval
&
Renaissance
Music

Derrick Henry

DEDICATION

To my wonderful family and friends,
whose unflagging support through every crisis
kept me going.

BLANDFORD PRESS

POOLE   DORSET

First published in the UK in 1983 by
Blandford Press
Link House, West Street
Poole, Dorset BH15 1LL

British Library Cataloguing in Publication Data
Henry, Derrick
The listener's guide to medieval and renaissance music
1. Music—History and criticism—Medieval, 400–1500
2. Music—History and criticism—16th century
I. Title
780′.9031   ML172

ISBN 0 7137 1353 4

The Listener's Guide to Medieval and Renaissance Music
was produced and prepared by
Quarto Marketing Ltd.
212 Fifth Avenue, New York, New York 10010

Editor: **Gene Santoro**
Editorial Assistant: **Richard Selman**
Designer: **Abby Kagan**

Typesetting: BPE Graphics, Inc.
Printed and bound in the United States by
the Maple Vail Group.

ACKNOWLEDGMENTS

Anyone who has attempted any sort of large-scale research project well
realizes that such undertakings could never be completed without the
efforts and resources of many people. I can't begin to publicly thank all
those in some way responsible for seeing me through this book. Their
anonymity in no way lessens my appreciation. But a select group of
people must be acknowledged, those whose advice, assistance, and
encouragement in countless ways shaped the final result. They are:
Mitchell Brauner, Maria Fowler, Rhona Freeman, Roland Jackson,
Richard Jensen, James Keller, William Malloch, Nancy Miller, Virginia
Mosser, Edward Nowacki, Claude Palisca, Henry Rasof, Joshua Rifkin,
Craig Wright, William F. Russell and the Pomona College Music Library,
and Eliza Thomas and the Harvard Music Library. The American periodicals *Commonweal* and *Record Review* generously allowed me to adapt a
number of articles written for them. Thanks too to Sedgwick Clark for
involving me in this project, to my expert editor Gene Santoro for
steering delicately between prodding and patience in the face of a very
tight schedule, and to my copyeditor, Thomas Matrullo, whose many
thoughtful suggestions added much.

CONTENTS

Introduction

While most of us have at least a passing familiarity with the magnificent art and literature of the Middle Ages and Renaissance, the music of these eras, is far less well known. Yet it is every bit as great. Its beauties are substantial and manifold, and will readily reveal themselves to anyone willing to make the effort.

This, I think, is ample justification for writing what is probably the first guide to recordings of medieval and Renaissance music. My goal is straightforward enough: to steer the reader via a combination of history, analysis, and actual sound through the evolution and development of Western music up to the end of the Renaissance. I address such basic questions as: What were the major styles? Who were the most important composers? What roles did various countries, institutions, and individuals play in the creation of a uniquely Western music? How was medieval and Renaissance music performed? Why is it worth listening to today, and what recordings form the best introduction to an understanding of it?

The organization is simplicity itself. The chapters proceed in roughly chronological order, each supplying historical background on a major repertoire followed by a discussion of important recordings of that repertoire. The Renaissance section is preceded by a brief overview of the entire period. No formal music background is necessary to understand what I have written I hope the book will win many converts to medieval and Renaissance music, and I fancy that readers who already listen to this music regularly may discover something new and useful in it as well.

Before the invention and refinement of recording, such a listener's guide would have served little purpose. There was plenty of reading material on the music, to be sure, but the opportunities to actually experience it were few and far between. And those performances that did occasionally crop up—on record or off—were generally of such poor quality that no one could legitimately censure those who built up an antipathy to early music. Today, with the easy availability of many pieces in excellent recorded performances, we can piece together a vivid aural picture of both our link with oral traditions and the emergence of peculiarly Western musical forms and practices. At last the astounding richness of medieval and Renaissance music, for so long silent, can begin to be appreciated anew.

Now we can hear first-rate performances of early music, often played on period instruments, on a tremendous variety of labels. Literally dozens of professional artists from all over the Western world are devoting their attention to these periods. Many musicians of formidable skill are even concentrating exclusively on early music. I would go so far as to say that it is among practitioners of early music that one may consistently find the most informed, creative, and stimulating music-making to be heard today.

As anyone who has compiled a discography well realizes, records come and go out of the catalogs with alarming alacrity.

If you do wait until a record is deleted all is not lost, however; there are a number of shops specializing in used records and in brand new cut-outs (see the guide to sources). For these reasons I have felt free to discuss any recordings of importance, whether or not they are currently available either in the US or UK.

Some readers may be surprised by the amount of space I have allotted to medieval music. This is not out of any prejudice against the Renaissance, which after all is arguably the richest period in the entire history of Western music, but rather because the Middle Ages provided all the basic materials for Renaissance composers. Without such medieval accomplishments as the development of clear pitch notation and the creation of measured rhythm, Western music as we now know it could not exist. And by clarifying exactly what those accomplishments entailed, the contributions of Renaissance composers can be more easily and succinctly explained.

Musical performance is an endlessly engrossing topic. The farther one goes back in time, the greater the difficulty of knowing what the composer intended. In this respect, modern performers of Beethoven and Stravinsky have a relatively easy task: The composer has supplied detailed markings to tell how his music should go. Not so in the Middle Ages and Renaissance. Rarely are indications given for such basic considerations as the number and disposition of voices and instruments, the appropriate instrumentation, tempo and dynamics, or phrasing and articulation. In many early manuscripts the very pitches are in doubt. Those weary of squirming through still another mediocre rendition of Beethoven's Fifth Symphony or Tchaikovsky's First Piano Concerto might compare a few recorded versions of a medieval piece like the troubadour song *Kalenda maya* (see Chapter 2) to ascertain how much greater the interpretative options of early music are.

As a consequence, performers of this music cannot read a score at face value and expect to bring it to life; they must supply the missing information in an imaginative and compelling way. But they also have a responsibility to do so in an ''authentic'' manner: to approach medieval and Renaissance music through the instruments, techniques, and aesthetics of the time. Only in this way can we hope to understand the music as it was conceived. Because it is my feeling that a performance that is both musically sensitive and historically authentic will be superior to one that is merely sensitive, I have placed considerable emphasis upon performance practices. This provides a concrete means to assess not only those recordings discussed herein but any others as well.

In the course of preparing this guide I have been continuously astonished both by the incredible range and communicative power of medieval and Renaissance music and by the breathtaking virtuosity of many musicians now performing it. The same exciting prospect awaits the beginning listener. In the right hands, this centuries-old music is far more than historical curiosity: it becomes living art.

1

CHANT:
The Foundation of Western Music

Background

The early history of Western music is inseparable from that of the early Christian Church. For at least fifteen hundred years the Church dominated music just as it did life in general. And for a millennium the only music heard in the Church was vocal, specifically chant.

At its most basic, chant is simply the unaccompanied intoning of prose or poetry. Such lightly sung delivery of a text has several advantages over speech: it projects more strongly, aids retention, and is aesthetically more pleasing. Small wonder, then, that the use of chant in liturgical services can be traced back to the earliest civilizations.

But chant at its highest development represents something far more sophisticated than mere intonation of simple melodic formulas: the chant repertoire contains what may be the most subtle and elaborately worked-out melodies known to man. That this is so should not seem too surprising, for chant in its purest form is in fact unadulterated melody, devoid of counterpoint, harmony, or instrumental accompaniment. This alone is enough to make chant sound strange to modern ears, a strangeness compounded by a modal scale system different from our present-day major and minor keys, and by free rhythm, without a strong, regular pulse. Then, too, chant is not music for music's sake; rather, it is strictly utilitarian. Each of the numerous subcategories of chant were designed to fulfill some specific role in the Catholic liturgy. Heard outside this context, chant cannot possibly achieve its full force.

Yet even when heard on record in the home, far removed from its intended setting, medieval chant can produce a powerful effect, as sizable record sales attest. The formal asceticism and profound reverence of chant may account for this popularity.

Chant, in style and in spirit, represents a world far removed from the hectic concerns of the here-and-now.

Influences

Chant was viewed by the Church Fathers on the one hand as a tremendous evangelical aid and on the other as a dangerous temptation towards the sybaritic. The latter fear was not unwarranted. The earliest Christians were for the most part Jews both by heritage and nationality, and, moreover, Jews living under Roman rule in a cosmopolitan world amidst Greco-Roman and Asian cultural traditions. By the Christian era Roman music (and much Asian music) was distinctly secular in nature, a source of spectacle and popular entertainment, associated with dancing, drinking, gourmandizing, and lustful pursuits. Understandably, neither the Jews nor the Christians wished to have anything to do with Roman merrymaking. This antipathy to all things Roman likewise explains the Jewish and Christian aversion to instrumental music. Instruments figure prominently in the Old Testament, but were banished without exception from the synagogue as a gesture of mourning over the Roman destruction of the Second Temple in 70 AD. Yet documentation of the presence of instruments at certain religious observances and their championing by some of the Church Fathers testify that the elimination of instruments in the services was far from complete.

One of the great mysteries of music history is how the organ, which had been an exclusively secular instrument, in the years 900-1200 AD comes to be almost entirely associated with the Church. After all, the pagan associations of the instrument would seem to mitigate against their use for religious purposes. Moreover, these early medieval organs were generally monstrous in size, raucous in sound, and exceedingly awkward in operation (sliders had to be pulled in and out manually, often requiring two players to encompass the instrument's full range, while the bellows usually necessitated several strong men to pump them). Still, the organ did become the major church instrument (though it never did receive official sanction), largely, it seems, through the efforts of the Benedictine order. The organ's original church function has yet to be satisfactorily resolved. Probably it was used primarily as a solo instrument, rarely as accompaniment to soloists or choirs.

While in the best interests of the early Christians to separate themselves from the practices of Romans, Jews, or any non-Christians, wholesale escape from their environment was obviously impossible. Higini Anglès in *The New Oxford History of Music* neatly summarizes the whole complex of formative relationships upon Christian chant when he observes that though "next to nothing is known of European popular song during the first thousand years of the Christian era ... beneath the Gregorian [Roman] repertory there lies a substratum of the most ancient religious and popular chant of both Eastern and Western derivation."

Early Chant

The overriding problem in studying Christian chant during its inception and first flowering is the same as with music of the ancient world: hardly anything survives. At the beginning of the

7th century Isidore of Seville observes: "If music is not retained by man's memory, it is lost, since it cannot be written down."

One decisive factor in determining the shape Western chant would take was the fact that in 330 Constantine moved his capital from Rome to Byzantium. This decision led to the formal division of the Christian world into Greek-speaking Eastern Orthodox and Western Latin-speaking Roman Catholic in the year 395. Now the Western branches were freed to organize their own independent liturgy. As a consequence the Mass became the most musically important rite in the West, the Office in the East.

The following picture emerges. During the early centuries of the Christian era every community (or even individual church) of any consequence developed its own localized rites and chant repertoire, which they passed on orally from generation to generation. Among the more prominent branches were the Byzantine (Byzantium, renamed Constantinople), Celtic (Ireland), Gallican (France), Mozarabic (Spain), Beneventan (lower Italy), Ambrosian (Milan), and—most important for the future of Western music—Gregorian (Rome).

Aside from the isolated 3rd century hymn, the earliest notated Christian chants of any sort date from the 8th century. Notation became necessary for several reasons. As the centuries passed and the liturgy grew increasingly large and complex, it proved more and more difficult (and time-consuming) to memorize all the chants. Moreover, Pepin (c. 714-768) and his son Charlemagne (742-814), the Frankish kings, deemed it politically expedient to adopt a consistent liturgy and chant repertoire throughout their kingdoms. They decided in favor of the Gregorian branch, centered in Rome, seat of the papacy. There consequently followed a long and painful conversion of local to Gregorian rites, one that undoubtedly effected the assimilation of many of these local elements, most importantly the Gallican and Ambrosian, into the Gregorian repertoire. (The Ambrosian liturgy was in fact never successfully suppressed, while the Mozarabic repertoire remained largely unaffected, Spain being outside Frankish jurisdiction.) Such standardization was, of course, impossible without some manner of clear and consistent notation.

Chant Notation

The earliest chant notation consisted of figures called *neumes* (Greek for "sign"). These dashes and dots, hooks and flourishes came to be inscribed above the liturgical text. While this staffless notation could unequivocally indicate the number, grouping, and syllable placement of tones as well as various ornamental subtleties, it could only show whether the melodic line was to ascend or descend; there was no means to specify the size of intervals between notes or the exact pitch level at which the chants were to be sung. At first this limitation was not particularly bothersome, for notation was conceived principally as a memory aid for singers who knew how the tune should go. However, the Frankish reforms necessitated a more accurate pitch notation, one that would allow standardization of a given melody (since each area tended to have its own variant). The solution was simple: draw a line, and arrange the pitches around it. But the further removed a pitch from that line, the more difficult it became for the scribe to notate and for the singer to decipher. So another line was added, then another, and still another, to form a total of four. Each line and space represented a step, just as they do in the five-line staff universally used today. The man generally credited with the introduction of four-line notation, as well as with various innovations simplifying the art of sight-singing, was a Benedictine monk known as Guido d'Arezzo (c. 990-1050). Keep in mind, however, that these notational advances did not spring overnight into full flower and universal practice as the result of one man's brilliant insights; the process was a slow one, and pitch notation did not reach its fullest development until well into the 12th century.

Chant Structure

Christian chant was not built upon the system of major and minor keys familiar to most of us from the music of the late Baroque through early 20th century. Rather there were eight ecclesiastical modes, identified by number, and grouped in pairs according to the *finalis* (generally the last note of a melody). Both modes I and II, for instance, would center around the finalis D. But mode I, the so-called *authentic* member of the pair, would focus in the range D-d, while mode II, the so-called *plagal* mode, would focus in the range A-a, a fourth lower. Similarly, both modes III and IV have a finalis E, but the authentic mode III focuses in the range E-e, the plagal mode IV in the range B-b.

As Donald Grout eloquently puts it in his *A History of Western Music*, "The particular quality of a mode is not merely a result of its range or its scale pattern of tones and semitones.... The concrete reality ... is to be found in the melodies themselves, the particular turns of phrase characteristic of each mode and each type of chant."

There evolved three principal means of realizing chants. These are: direct, responsorial, and antiphonal. Direct chants (such as *tracts*) are for a soloist or full choir. Responsorial chants (*graduals, alleluias, responds*), involve alternation between a soloist and chorus. Antiphonal chants (*antiphons, introits, offertories, communions*) alternate between two half–choruses. Note that some distinction was always preserved between a soloist, half-choir, and full choir. Too often nowadays these important distinctions are totally ignored, and the various types of chants are performed by full choir throughout.

Most chants are narrow in range, predominantly stepwise in motion, and unpredictable in contour, with a lack of regular rises and falls in the melodic line. Those readers desiring more detailed information concerning the manifold types of chants and their modal and formal structure are directed to the sources in my reading list, and—for the truly insatiable—to Willi Apel's *Gregorian Chant* (Indiana University Press, 1958).

Performance Practice

"Authentic" performance of Christian chant presents many problems. Foremost among them are vocal production, acoustic circumstances, disposition and constitution of the performing forces, instrumental practice, and rhythmic interpretation.

Chant was, of course, conceived for churches, not for concert halls, and relied upon resonant surroundings for its intended effect. The number of participants could vary enormously, depending on the occasion. Choirs of 100 men and boys were not unusual in 12th-century Milan for the larger feasts. For everyday services, far smaller choirs (typically four to eight) were the rule, if only from economic necessity. In Rome the choir would stand in a circle around the *praecentor* or director, who guided the singing through hand gestures. Some scholars contend that these *cheironomic* (after the Greek *cheir*, "hand") motions were used by the praecentor in the era before notation to convey to his choir not only rhythmic nuance but also the up-and-down contour of a melody. In Milan the various categories of musical personnel (priests, deacons, lectors, etc.) did not all stand together in a group, but were assigned specific positions in the cathedral, so that the overall impact owed much to spatial effects.

The choirs and soloists, originally drawn from members of the congregation, grew more professional as the challenge of learning and executing the chant repertoire grew more demanding. By the 5th century a Schola Cantorum was established in Rome expressly for the purpose of studying and performing liturgical chant. Under the guidance of Pope Gregory I (590-604) it was reorganized and expanded. During the period of Carolingian (Frankish) unification the Schola played a crucial role in assuring the standardization, preservation, and dissemination of chant, both through its missionary activities to churches and monasteries all over the Western Christian world and through its painstaking notation of the repertoire. Indispensable to the curriculum of the Schola and to the similar educational institutions which it inspired was the training of boys. Indeed, in Milan boys would often be called upon to sing the more difficult chants for the simple reason that they had spent more time rehearsing them and were thus better prepared.

In general the rule was that the sexes did not sing together. Women were excluded from musical involvement in Jewish ceremonies, a practice that St. Paul wholeheartedly endorsed: "The women shall be silent in the assemblies" (I *Corinthians* 14:34). As late as the 5th century, though, Isidore of Pelusium begrudgingly permitted women to sing in services on the supposition that they would otherwise spend their time in gossip. Choirs of nuns are found throughout the Christian era up to the present day. Nonetheless, the demise of mixed groups was foreordained by the establishment of the Schola Cantorum and its replacement of women with boys.

Christian chant was intended for unaccompanied voices. At times, however, and particularly on festive occasions, the choir would alternate with an organ (itself sometimes accompanied or supplanted by bells). This would prove especially effective with chants having regular versification, such as hymns and sequences. Very possibly the organist would embellish the bare monophonic melodic line. But these practices only emerged late in the Christian period: not until the 9th century is there unambiguous documentation of the use of an organ in the Church, and not until the 13th century does the organ appear to have regularly participated with the choir in Mass services.

Medieval vocal production remains a mystery. Almost assuredly singers did not cultivate the heavy vibrato normally heard in the performance of art music today. Whether they produced the pinched, nasal, vibrato-free tone that some musicologists have espoused is another matter. The goal apparently was to produce a beautiful sound, yet one uncontaminated by sensual appeal. Isidore of Seville (d. 636) described the ideal voice as "high (or bright), sweet and clear." St. Bernard of Clairvaux (c. 1090-1153) provided his monks with these precepts: "Let the chant be full of gravity; let it be neither worldly, nor too rude and poor . . . let it be sweet, yet without levity, and, while it please the ear let it move the heart."

Ornament and Improvisation
The contentious question of improvisation and embellishment will probably never be settled. Certain neumes (these appear principally in early manuscripts) are generally acknowledged to be abbreviations for various sorts of ornaments, just as today ⌇⌇ represents a shorthand for trill, and ∽ for melodic turn. Less clear is the extent to which *unspecified* notes were inserted into the performance of a melody. Embellishment of this sort, which could be either spontaneous or rehearsed, survived well into the Renaissance.

The chant repertoire was built upon a fluid oral tradition. This goes a long way toward explaining the existence of different versions of a given chant. These versions represent legitimate performing variations. A scribe at the very beginning of the notation era thus would not be preserving a universal model, but simply one of many performance possibilities. In doing so he might, in the words of the noted chant scholar Alejandro Planchart, "change, recast, expand, or entirely recompose the musical and literary texts received from an exemplar." Still, the very act of writing down a melody implied a preference for one realization over another and paved the way for eventual standardization. The primary function of these early manuscripts, in fact, appears to be not as books to sing from—they were far too tiny—but rather as archival sources designed to regulate the oral tradition and to assist the praecentor both in remembering the vast repertoire and in teaching it to his schola.

Rhythm
Of all the aspects of chant, rhythm has proven to be the most elusive. Since information bearing on this matter does not appear until well into the 9th century, deduction of the rhythmic realization of chant during its formative centuries can at best be highly speculative.

This said, two basic types of rhythmic ordering can be isolated: free and metric. Metric rhythm, the sort most familiar to the Western listener, presupposes the organization of notes into regularly recurring groupings. For example, in 2/4 meter every such grouping (called a measure or bar) will contain the equivalent of two quarter notes. A good deal of evidence suggests that chants with regularly recurrent verse structures, such as hymns and sequences, were performed in a metrical manner, with the clear, steady beat that this implies.

But the bulk of the chant repertoire probably was performed in "free" rhythm. Such rhythm also is organized by various groupings of notes, but these notes are not subjected to a uniform metric structure. Thus the equivalent of a 2/8 measure might be followed by a 3/8 measure, and continue varying in no regular pattern. The real issue, one which has incited heated controversy, is to ascertain the precise nature of this "free" rhythm.

A central question is the relative lengths of the individual notes. Some scholars, the so-called *equalists*, contend that each note has roughly the same rhythmic value, but without fixed meter. Others, loosely termed *measuralists*, say that notes of varying lengths freely alternate. This latter viewpoint admits two distinct possibilities: 1) the notes can be of indeterminate length, or 2) (the more widely held position) they can bear a strict *proportional* relationship to one another. The simplest such proportion would be 2 : 1. No matter which proportional system is adopted, the performer must still decide which notes receive the longer values and which the shorter.

The foremost equalist was Dom Joseph Pothier, a chant scholar at the Benedictine order of the Abbey of Solesmes. He proposed a system whereby the accents of the non-metrical Latin texts and the grouping of neumes determined the rhythmic organization, resulting in a declamatory style. Dom André Mocquerau, Pothier's student and successor as choral director at Solesmes, retained his teacher's equalist viewpoint but rejected textual rhythm, accent, and neumatic notation as rhythmic determinants. A chant melody, he maintained, had its own intrinsic rhythm, which may or may not coincide with that of the words. His theories, which called for an irregular succession of two- and three-note groups of equal notes, became codified into the so-called Solesmes method which has virtually monopolized chant performance up to the present day. The nature of rhythmic realization might also depend upon the nature of the musical setting, whether it is *syllabic* (one note for each syllable of text), *neumatic* (several syllables per note), or *melismatic* (many notes per syllable, as in an *Alleluia*). Logically, the more melismatic the chant, the more rhapsodic the rhythmic realization.

The Evolution of Chant Rhythm

A bit of historical perspective might help clarify these rhythmic issues. The early chant manuscripts contained a wealth of neume shapes and written information. The later manuscripts, from around the 12th century on, while infinitely more precise in matters of pitch, employ nondescript square notation. Assuming (as most recent scholarship does) that the early neumes possess rhythmic significance, their subsequent homogenization would reflect a fundamental change in rhythmic performance around the year 1100. Contemporary theorists for the most part confirm this view (though one should be wary of interpreting their writings at face value). For instance, Hucbald of St. Armand writes in the *Commemoratio brevis* from the first half of the 10th century: "All the longs must be equally long, all the shorts of equal brevity." Aribo Scholasticus in *De Musica* (c. 1070) informs his reader that "in the past not only the composers of chant but also the singers took great care to compose and sing everything in due proportion. But such a consideration has long since died; indeed it has been buried." On such evidence we can postulate that a proportional system of some form or another (not necessarily in a strict 2 : 1 relationship) was extensively practiced during the first millenium or so of Christian chant. But after that time a simpler performance method, one based more nearly on equal note values, took the fore.

The picture emerges of an evolution in rhythmic performance from something highly flexible, with the possibility for many spontaneous touches, to something substantially more fixed and straightlaced. This, however, must only be taken as a general trend occurring over a wide time span, for there is no reason to presume that chant performance reflected either a stable tradition or one based on systematic rhythmic procedures. As late as the 12th century St. Bernard of Clairvaux could write: "Take the antiphonal of Rheims and compare it with that of Soissons, Amiens, or Beauvais; if, beginning with the first page, you find any similarity, render homage unto God."

SELECTED RECORDINGS

By the time of the Renaissance the hallowed traditions of chant performance had begun to decline sharply. Not until the mid-19th century were efforts made to return to the chant manuscripts and restore the beauty of these venerable melodies to their original glory. The impetus for this task was provided by the Abbey of Solesmes monk Dom Prosper Guéranger and carried out by the next generation of Solesmes scholars. So impressed was the Vatican by these efforts that with the *Motu Proprio* of 1903 they sanctioned a series of chant publications incorporating the Solesmes research. Through these influential publications, Dom Mocquereau's theories acquired their monopoly on chant performance. In skilled hands, this so-called Solesmes method has proven capable of extraordinarily subtle and satisfying results. But examined under the sometimes harsh light of modern scholarship, the Solesmes work manifests severe shortcomings.

For one thing, the Solesmes editions are based on collations of the chant repertoire. Most chants survive in several manuscripts, with each version a bit (and sometimes more than a bit) different than the other. The Solesmes scholars compared all the available variants and extracted from them a composite which they perceived as the ideal form of that chant. But what they ended up with was, as often as not, a chant melody that *did not actually exist* in any source—in other words, a hybrid. Then, too, justification for the Solesmes performance method is historically skewed. It relies heavily on the statements of late medieval theorists while glossing over the sometimes contradictory evidence of the early theorists, as if a single performance tradition held for the entire Christian period. In addition, certain neumes from the older manuscripts are interpreted by the Solesmes monks as mere lengthenings of notes rather than as the ornamental directions they are now known to represent.

SUNDAY VESPERS/COMPLINE
Peters PLE-047
GOOD FRIDAY
Peters PLE-108
Both with Monks' Choir of the Abbey of Saint-Pierre de Solesmes conducted by Dom Joseph Gajard

All criticisms aside, the Solesmes method has almost single-handedly served to resurrect and sustain a viable performing style of the Gregorian chant literature, and therefore deserves pride of place in any discussion of the recorded repertoire. A logical starting point is the many recordings of the Solesmes monastery choir under Dom Joseph Gajard, their director from 1914-71. The Sunday Vespers and Compline album is of special interest, as it documents a live service. More polished if less atmospheric is the Good Friday album, which features a powerful cantillation of the St. John Passion. One striking aspect of this performance is the way in which pitch and tempo serves to dramatize the characters: low and slow for Christ, high and fast for the crowd of Jews, and somewhere in between for the Evangelist. This was standard medieval practice; expressive directions of this sort appear in manuscripts from as early as the 9th century.

Any of Gajard's recordings admirably illustrate the flowing, reverent style cultivated by the Solesmes monks, an approach which Mary Berry has aptly described as characterized by "the smooth expressive legato with its undoubted 'spiritual' quality—enhanced by the enveloping resonance of the building—the firm syllabic emission, the lifted accents, and the softening of the melodic peaks which gives the style its extraordinary elasticity."

TRADITION OF THE GREGORIAN CHANT
Various choirs from Spain, Switzerland, Italy, Germany, and France
DG Archiv 2723-071 (six records, also available singly)

The practices promulgated by Gajard and his choir, both through performance and the guidelines contained in the *Méthode de Solesmes*, have served as a norm to be adopted or opposed by monastic choirs throughout the Western Christian world. A valuable overview of the divergent performance styles to be heard in various monasteries (from Switzerland, Spain, Italy, France, and Germany) as well as of the different liturgical forms and chant repertoires, is contained in Archiv's boxed set entitled "Tradition of the Gregorian Chant." This title is something of a misnomer, since one of the more interesting albums in the set is devoted to Ambrosian (Milanese) chant, which has a more Eastern, less austere flavor than its Roman counterpart, and another includes a striking selection of Mozarabic chants. Unfortunately, for all its documentary value, several albums in this Archiv collection are marred by singing that leaves much to be desired in terms of accuracy, togetherness, and tonal beauty—problems affecting even the best of monastic choirs to one degree or another.

A GUIDE TO GREGORIAN CHANT
Vanguard VSD 71217
TENTH-CENTURY LITURGICAL CHANT IN PROPORTIONAL RHYTHM
Nonesuch H-71348
PLAINCHANT AND POLYPHONY FROM MEDIEVAL GERMANY
Nonesuch H-71312
All with the Schola Antiqua, R. John Blackley, director

One happy consequence of the reforms of the Second Vatican Council has been to free the way for greater experimentation in chant performance. Non-church choirs have gotten into the act.

One such group, R. John Blackley's Schola Antiqua, has been expressly founded for the purpose of "the study and performance of Gregorian Chant in proportional, equalist, and metrical rhythm. Very many of its chants are newly transcribed; all are presented in its own performing editions." Blackley's singers are professionals. In both his London (Vanguard) and New York (Nonesuch) ensembles the unanimity, virtuosity, and delicious sensuousness of the vocalism beggar description. Some might even find these performances *too* passionate and dramatic for liturgical purposes. But the clarity, vitality, and telling musicianship of Blackley's records are hard to resist.

On the Vanguard album a number of the chants are enhanced by the use of the excellent Trinity Whitgift School Boys' Choir. In the hymn *Iste confessor* the boys sing the verses, and all forces join together for the refrains. Equally effective is the antiphon *Salve regina*, where after the solo incipit the men and boys alternate for each line of text until the final line, when both choruses come together.

Though all but three of the chants on this Vanguard disc are sung in equalist rhythm, there are a number of important interpretive departures from the Solesmes method. Squiggly neumes known as *quilismas* are not performed by simply extending the duration of the note, as in the Solesmes tradition, but are realized as the mordent-like turn modern scholar holds was intended. Similarly, repeated notes are not tied together as one long note in the Solesmes fashion, but rather are articulated as individual entities in their own right. This articulation leads to a finished product surprisingly different from the norm, most strikingly in the offertory *Jubilate Deo universa terra,* whose melody is in fact built upon numerous thrice-repeated notes. Further, the unusually free approach to equalist rhythm taken by the Schola Antiqua produces some distinctive consequences: listen to the way Blackley's almost jazzlike rendering of the solo in the alleluia *Adest una* contrasts with the highly rhythmic execution of the choral sections of the chant.

Three of the chants Blackley has selected are not executed in an equalist manner. The two hymns are given metrical readings in which the accents are determined by the long and short syllabification of the classical Latin poetry. This is thought to be the way such hymns were sung up to the 5th century. Finally, there is one example of proportional singing, that of the introit *Rorate coeli.* All three nonequalist examples are highly convincing, and audibly different in effect from the Solesmes method. They provide the best possible argument for alternative styles of performing Gregorian chant.

While I urge acquisition of *A Guide to Gregorian Chant* as the finest single introduction to the possibilities of chant performance, Blackley's *Tenth-Century Liturgical Chant* is still more fascinating. It contains a Mass for Christmas Day sung by a men's schola and a Mass for Easter Sunday sung by a women's schola, both drawn from Laon MS 239 (c. 930), one of the oldest surviving chant books. All these chants are sung in proportional rhythm. Moreover, Blackley's singers adopt an extremely liberal attitude toward *liquescent* (ornamental) neumes, extending as far as startling microtonal slides. Comparison of these proportional renditions with equalist ones of the same chants on Blackley's other albums (or those by monastic groups) makes for a fascinating experience. In general, the use of proportional methods in speechlike recitation passages strikes me as stilted, but their application to the chant melodies proper produces musical results of great complexity. Perhaps partially for this reason, I find the proportional realizations sustain my interest over longer time periods than the familiar Solesmes approach. Moreover, they emerge as not all forced, but rather surprisingly natural—minus the mannerisms which have accrued in Solesmes performance over the years.

OXFORD ANTHOLOGY OF MUSIC: SACRED MONOPHONY
Pro Cantione Antiqua directed by Edgar Fleet
Peters PLE 114
HYMNS, SEQUENCES, RESPONSORIES, 400-1400
Capella Antiqua of Munich, Konrad Ruhland, director
RCA Seon RL 30383 or Telefunken Der Alte Werk 6.41213

Brief mention should be given to other professional organizations pursuing alternative methods of chant performance. Konrad Ruhland, with a contingent of eight men from his Capella Antiqua of Munich, devotes an entire disc to the metrical realization of a millenium's worth of hymns, sequences, and responsories. The singing is clear, firm-toned, and lively. A fine selection of Gallican, Mozarabic, and Gregorian chant is presented on the Pro Cantione Antiqua's generous offering, which also features a persuasive version of *The Play of Herod*. Like the Schola Antiqua, the 14 men in the Pro Cantione try a variety of performance styles (including several not in the Schola Antiqua's albums), and execute them all with compelling virtuosity and tonal beauty. Highly recommended.

A FEATHER ON THE BREATH OF GOD: SEQUENCES AND HYMNS BY ABBESS HILDEGARD OF BINGEN
Gothic Voices directed by Christopher Page
Hyperion A66039

Hildegard of Bingen (1098–1179) emerges as one of the most remarkable and fascinating creative personalities of the entire medieval period, and one of the first women whose music has been preserved in any quantity. She was, among other things, an abbess, naturalist, playwright (she wrote the first morality play), poetess, and visionary. So celebrated were her prophecies that she was sought out by popes, emperors, kings, archbishops, and all manner of lesser mortals. Her melodies are wider in range and contain larger intervals than is customary in Gregorian chant. They manifest a mystical intensity, spontaneous character, and often haunting beauty. These qualities are admirably captured by the Gothic Voices's dramatically shaped, superbly sung performances, some by a small group of men, some by a small group of women, and two in unaccompanied solo renditions from the extremely impressive contralto Margaret Philpot. All reflect equalist rhythmic precepts. Only distracting instrumental drones added to half of the eight chants mar the proceedings.

ALLELUIAS AND OFFERTORIES OF THE GAULS
Iegor Reznikoff, cantor
Harmonia Mundi HM 1044

EASTER ON MOUNT ATHOS

Monks of the Xenophontos Monastery, Mount Athos, directed by
Abbot Alexios
DG Archiv 2533-413, 2533-443, 2533-446

Finally, I list two recordings with a decidedly non-Western
flavor. In the first, the Russian Iegor Reznikoff attempts to
recapture the sound and techniques of a 6th-century Christian
cantor through study of early notation and through comparative
listening to present-day solo cantors of other religions with even
more ancient and unbroken traditions behind them: Jewish,
Islamic, Hindu, Buddhist, etc. The results are mesmeric and
exciting, even if we have no way of determining how closely they
represent the practices of a bygone era. Unfortunately, Harmonia Mundi supplies very little hard information on the justification
for Reznikoff's decisions (including the use of a drone). Archiv's
three-record presentation, *Easter on Mount Athos*, documents a
live performance of an authentic Greek Orthodox service. The
product of a Byzantine tradition, the music-making is far bolder
and more improvisatory than Gregorian chant performance as
brought down to us by the Solesmes monks. The Greek monks
make free use of bells and drones and sing with a harsher tone
than their Western counterparts. Though it is only conjecture,
such a style might actually be closer to that practiced in the early
centuries of Western Christendom than the dignified but ever-
so-polite chanting of the Solesmes choir and their disciples.

2

THE SPREAD OF MONOPHONY

The elaboration of monophonic music took two primary forms in the high Middle Ages: dramatic and lyrical. We shall first take up the development of medieval drama, sacred and secular, and then trace the rise of monophonic song as practiced by the troubadours, trouvères, and their contemporaries.

From Chant to Drama

By the 9th century the Mass liturgy had become firmly established. Inevitably Church composers began experimenting with ways to enrich it. These experiments began in the form of long, flowing musical phrases called melismas appended after various chants, especially *Alleluias*. The next step was to fit a non-liturgical text to such a melisma, the better to remember its elaborate melody. By the early 10th century these techniques reached their logical conclusion: new words *and* music were composed as a sort of commentary to be inserted into the Mass. This additive process, in whatever form, is called *troping*.

Troping, a product of the creative interaction between music and text, was to assume great importance for another art: drama. Tropes to the *Introits* for Christmas and Easter were commonly written in a question and answer, or dialogue, format. Gradually this dialogue was expanded until eventually entire scenes were added, replete with Biblical characters and incidents. Because of their length, these theatrical creations became detached from the Mass and transferred to new positions in the service, most commonly between Matins and Lauds. David Hughes in *A History of European Music* describes the development admirably: "Members of the clergy were assigned parts and given costumes; a section of the church was set aside as the scene and furnished with appropriate properties; and the singers made suitable motions and gestures while singing their parts. This was in fact the beginning of modern European drama. . . . "

Liturgical Drama

The repertoires of liturgical drama, as these works came to be known, quickly expanded. Favorite subjects were the miracles of various saints (especially St. Nicolas) and well-known Biblical stories such as Daniel in the lions' den, Herod's massacre of the innocents, and the wise and foolish virgins.

Little attempt at either characterization or motivation are evident in the scripts of liturgical drama. The acting style, judging from the often extremely detailed stage directions, was restrained and highly formalized. Though both male and female roles were normally included, generally all these were played by persons of a single sex. Even nuns were fond of performing. Not surprisingly, this new art form became extremely popular. As Paul Henry Lang tells it in his *Music in Western Civilization,* "Men and women, students and monks, rogues and noblemen, peasants and burghers were all eager spectators." One suspects that their interest in the theatre was not completely pious.

Vernacular Drama

As time went on, participation was extended to include laymen as well as clergy. This increasing secularization manifested itself in the tunes as well, which occasionally took on a popular air. Concurrent with the development of liturgical drama, which was in Latin and entirely sung, was that of vernacular drama, spoken plays with incidental music. Though the exact relationship of liturgical to vernacular drama has been hotly debated, it is apparent that many of the early vernacular plays were an outgrowth of the church dramas. Indeed, Biblical subjects form the greater part of the surviving vernacular repertoire. Most famous are the so-called mystery or miracle plays. These might portray scenes from the life of Jesus, the Acts of the Apostles, or the Creation, to name just a few prominent subjects. All the vernacular plays were performed outside the church under secular sponsorship, often by professional actors. Initially clerics participated too, but this practice was halted by a papal edict issued in 1210 forbidding the clergy from acting on a public stage.

Music and Drama

Liturgical dramas are for the most part sung to actual chants or chant-derived melodies. These are preserved in chant notation, without clear indication of rhythm. Thus, there is every reason to presume that these melodies were rendered in a manner fundamentally similar to that of liturgical chant [see Chapter 1].

The function of music differed depending upon whether the drama was liturgical or vernacular. In liturgical drama it was essential, as all the words were sung. In vernacular plays it was incidental, although often substantial: music, whether vocal or instrumental, might serve for preludes, postludes, and interludes, processions, fanfares, and dances, but could always be eliminated without affecting the story line. These plays might be viewed as the medieval equivalents of the Broadway musical, while liturgical drama is the medieval equivalent of opera. A central error in the modern recreation of liturgical drama results from the confusion between these separate performance traditions. This applies both to presentation style, which would naturally be more contemporary and less formal in the vernacular drama, and to the insertion of incidental music, which apparently played little part in liturgical dramas.

The Role of Instruments

For the great majority of liturgical plays there is a complete absence of instructions pertaining to instrumental participation. Even those works that are explicitly detailed in most aspects of stage production tend to be stingy in their instrumental directives. Evidently the chief function of the instrumental music in the liturgical dramas was to accompany movement of the characters from one place to another. One of the grandest of all these works, the early 13th-century *Play of Daniel* (written by students at the Beauvais cathedral school), contains a large number of processional numbers, all with texts. Yet even here only a single mention is made of instruments in the stage directions. The conclusion seems inescapable: "Neither text nor liturgical tradition supports the idea of lavish and continuous musical accompaniment" (John Stevens in *The New Grove*). For most productions of liturgical drama, which after all took place within the confines of the church and the liturgy, the only appropriate instruments were those that might occasionally play a part in the service proper: organ and bells.

Vernacular drama outside the Church was another matter. Musicians might be drawn from a town's own resources, or hired from outside; many of these plays were presented by professional traveling companies. Here, then, was an opportunity to utilize a wide and colorful range of instruments, as many as circumstances dictated. After all, these vernacular plays were designed—unlike the liturgical dramas—as entertainment first and foremost.

Virtually all the vernacular dramas surviving with music are on religious subjects; the most important portion of this music is chant. Of those plays based on secular topics, only one comes down to us with a substantial amount of its music intact. *Robin et Marion* by Adam de la Halle (c. 1237–c. 1287), last, and some say greatest of the trouvères, was written around 1283 while Adam was in the service of Robert II, Count of Artois. *Robin* is a lighthearted aristocratic entertainment in which a dramatized *pastourelle* (a type of ballad portraying an amorous encounter between a knight on the make and a shepherdess, with her inevitable rescue by a manly shepherd) gets embellished by songs and dances featuring a group of shepherds as well as the central characters. The 16 tunes dispersed throughout the spoken text were probably not composed by Adam himself since they are of a popular nature, and set down—in contrast to Adam's own monophonic *chansons* (songs)—in metrical notation.

By the 14th century the heyday of liturgical drama was over, having been superceded by the more spectacular and accessible vernacular plays. These, with their easily understandable language and spoken dialogue, form the true beginning of European drama.

From Drama to Lyric

The close interrelationship between the sacred and secular in the Middle Ages has already been remarked upon. It can be seen both in the Biblical topics constituting the majority of vernacular plays and in the use of popular tunes in liturgical dramas and chant melodies with secular texts. *Las Cantigas de Santa María*, the foremost collection of Spanish monophonic song, consists of religious poetry conceived for court performance and reflects an enormous diversity of musical styles. And an important group of liturgical dramas is contained in the *Carmina burana*, the most comprehensive medieval collection of Latin secular lyrics (a tradition which dates back as far as the 6th century).

Carmina Burana

Carmina burana (known today primarily through Carl Orff's cantata which uses several of its poems as texts) is an anthology compiled shortly after the middle of the 13th century. Probably the title translates *Songs of Benediktbeuern*, after the monastery where the manuscript was assembled. The composition of a wealthy cleric or aristocrat who took pleasure in the poetry, it numbers more than 200 poems of wide-ranging content and character, carefully ordered according to four main groups: 1) the liturgical dramas, just mentioned; 2) moral and satirical songs (laments on the lowering of moral standards, observations on the state of the world, etc.); 3) love songs; and 4) songs of eating, drinking, gambling, and the like. The poetry for the most part originated in France during the late 11th and 12th centuries. Much of it was written by students who moved from one school to the next before it became customary to establish residency at a university, or by clerics who had either broken their vows or were not content with a monastic existence. These vagabonds were called *goliards*. Though intelligent and learned, they were given to parody, satire, and every kind of amusement. Many of their poems are couched in language of an irreverent and even blasphemous and obscene nature. Although most of them were conceived as songs, unfortunately those provided with music appear in a notation that is largely indecipherable. Thus we are dependent on later sources with legible notation for a sense of what they should sound like. Yet there is enough evidence to confirm that the music mirrors the poetry in its diversity.

Bards

The greatest contributions to medieval secular music came not from the goliards, but rather from jongleurs, minstrels, and troubadours, all at least having indirectly evolved from that prototype of a poet-singer, the bard. Bards may readily be traced to antiquity, Homer (before 700 BC) being the most famous. They would perform lengthy epics or narrative tales to melodic lines, the character and complexity of which remains obscure. Music served a secondary, not a dominant, function: to enhance the tale and clarify its formal structure.

Unlike the peripatetic scholars and clerics, medieval bards were by and large an uneducated lot, and therefore performed in the vernacular rather than in Latin. From at least the 10th century, bards in northern France cultivated epic poems known as *chansons de geste* (songs of deeds), extended creations with many stanzas of irregular length. The best-known of these chansons is the *Song of Roland*, which in its modern form took shape (probably at the hands of several people) over the last decades of the 11th century. None of the music of the *chansons de geste* (or for that matter of any other bardic poetry) has been preserved.

Jongleurs and Minstrels

In order to survive, nomadic poet-musicians were forced to develop a variety of skills. These generally were of the theatrical sort we associate today with the circus: juggling, acrobatics, animal training, and the like.

Such jack-of-all-trades entertainers were known as *jongleurs*. But many of these jongleurs focused their talents on music, eventually forming themselves into guilds. Thus during the bulk of the Middle Ages "jongleur" could refer to a professional entertainer of the most general description, or to what for all purposes was a professional musician in the modern sense. By the early 14th century this latter group was often distinguished by the term minstrel *(ménestrel)*.

Minstrels might be self-employed itinerant musicians (in which cases other entertainment skills might come in handy), or they might be attached to a particular household or court. It is the latter whose presence is most fully documented. No women are listed on the rosters of court musicians.

Troubadours and Trouvères

In contrast to jongleurs and minstrels, the troubadours, trouvères, and their derivatives were essentially creative artists.

Simply stated, troubadours and trouvères were poet-composers flourishing in France during the 12th and 13th centuries to whom we owe the creation of the first great body of Western vernacular song. The troubadours worked in southern France (then Provence) and wrote in Provençal, the *langue d'oc;* the trouvères, active a bit later, worked in the north and wrote in old French, the *langue d'oïl*. Some 2600 troubadour poems have been preserved, of which music survives for not quite 300; some 1700 of the 2400 extant trouvère poems come down with accompanying mélodies. All the music is monophonic. Composers of courtly monophony differed from bards in several fundamental respects. Music and poetry were (at least at first) pastimes, not sources of livelihood. Their poems were almost entirely lyric, rather than epic or narrative, in content. Their poetry was shorter, and of a technical accomplishment far surpassing that of most bardic literature. There are still other differences. Though typically serious, well-educated, and sophisticated verse-technicians, this literacy did not necessarily extend to music. Consequently, as often as not, troubadours (here used in the generic sense to include all composers of courtly monody, from whatever country) hired jongleurs to execute their songs. There was another reason for this practice: public performance was regarded as unbecoming a nobleman, accepting money unthinkable. So while a troubadour with aristocratic pretensions might not hesitate to sing his latest creations for a group of his friends, public dissemination demanded professional performers.

Though most of the composers of the pieces discussed so far in this book have remained anonymous, a fair amount is known about the troubadours and their followers. Some 460 troubadours have been identified, and of these music by 42 has survived. Many had high social standing. The first troubadour whose poems have been preserved, Guillaume IX of Aquitaine (1071–1126) was a duke and a count. Thibaut IV of Champagne (1201–53), an early trouvère, was the unscrupulous King of Navarre. On the other hand, if the early troubadours and trouvères tended to be aristocratic amateurs of both sexes with ample leisure time for creating their songs, the greatest contri-

In this lovely early 17th century engraving by Gregorius Fentzel, an allegorical scene is depicted which displays lutes, trumpets, viola da gamba, shawms, and harps.

bution to this new art stems from the professionals in noble employ. These men began their careers as jongleurs, but rose to the rank of troubadour by virtue of their talent. The troubadour Marcabru (d. c. 1147), famed as a misogynist, was reputedly a foundling, and Bernart de Ventadorn (fl. 1145–95), regarded by his contemporaries as the finest poet among the troubadours, was the son of a baker. Women, too, figured prominently in the movement, not only as poetic subject matter and through their patronage, but as creators of poetry in their own right. Some 20 women troubadours are known by name; Béatrix, the Countess of Die (late 12th c.), is the only one to have a song preserved with music.

The Diffusion of Troubadour Art

The troubadour/trouvère movement eventually extended far beyond France. The Crusades were not the only factor responsible for spreading the fame of troubadour art; royal intermarriage was another. Eleanor of Acquitaine (c. 1122–1204) is the most conspicuous example. Her love of troubadour art is not surprising: her grandfather was Guillaume IX; her father, Guillaume X, though not a troubadour, was exceedingly active as a patron. Eleanor carried on the family tradition during her first marriage (1137–52) to King Louis VII of France (1120–80). Her flirtations evidently did not set well with Louis, who had their marriage annulled in 1152. Eleanor immediately remarried, this time to the soon-to-be King Henry II of England. Her son Richard-the-Lion-Hearted (1157–1199) was a practicing troubadour, and later King of England.

A third factor in the diffusion of troubadour art was the religious and political war between the Catholic nobles and the heretical nobility of Provence (Languedoc) known as the Albigensian Crusade (1209–29). After this bloodbath, which virtually annihilated the brilliant culture of Provence, many troubadours fled France.They established themselves throughout Europe, and so led to a flowering of courtly monody in Italy (hardly any music survives), England (very little music remains, though we do have several songs by Richard the Lion-Hearted), in Portugal and in Spain (little purely secular monophony has been preserved, though there is that great collection of *Cantigas de Santa María*), and in Germany (the *minnesinger* movement flourishing in the 12th–14th centuries). By far the most widespread and long-lived of these various offshoots was that of the *minnesingers*. Their strong reliance upon troubadour/trouvère models of courtly love may be discerned from their very name: *Minne* meant "love," thus a minnesinger was a singer of love poetry. Minnesinger songs tend to be jumpier in melodic outline than their French counterparts and also, thanks to the accentual nature of German poetry, more metrical rhythmically. Among the foremost minnesingers were Wolfram von Eschenbach (fl. c. 1200), author of the epic poem *Parzival;* Walther von der Vogelweide (c. 1170–1228), later immortalized in Wagner's *Die Meistersinger;* the knight Neidhart von Reuenthal (c. 1190–after 1236); and Heinrich von Meissen (d. 1318), called *Frauenlob* because he advocated the use of *Frau* (lady) instead of the more common *Weib* (woman).

Monophonic song eventually gave way to the new art of polyphony, music with more than one part (see Chapter 4). Yet monody did not die out until well into the Renaissance and beyond. Guillaume Machaut, the most famous French composer of the 14th century, wrote large numbers of monophonic songs; the same is true of Oswald von Wolkenstein (c. 1377–1445), the most famous German composer of the late Middle Ages.

Troubadour Poetry and Music

The finest troubadour/trouvère poetry ranks among the most subtle and original of its age. Generally these songs (chansons) are cast in strophic form, with the same rhyme scheme and melody for each stanza. Within each stanza, however, can lie a wealth of structural patterns. For their subject matter, the poets concentrated on courtly, courteous love in all its manifestations. This reflected the elevated status of women within an increasingly court-dominated society. But the importance of the new feminine ideal should not be overemphasized. Notes Richard Hoppin in his recent book *Medieval Music:* "The striking contrast between the variety of forms and the sameness of themes in troubadour poetry clearly shows that what mattered was not the subject itself but the manner of its presentation."

Music was a crucial element in that presentation. In the words of Theodore Karp in *The New Grove*, "Neither the troubadours nor the trouvères regarded their poetry as a self-sufficient art. Their verse achieved life mainly through the performance of the singer. Indeed, Folquet de Marseille (c. 1150–1231) wrote that 'a verse without music is a mill without water.' '' But though music was a crucial aspect of this art, the relationship between tune and text was not inseparable in, say, the manner of a Schubert song. Rarely did the melodic form correspond precisely to the rhyme pattern of the verse; it could hardly be expected to, given the intricacy and variety of poetic structure within each stanza, all adaptable to a single melody. The music itself draws inspiration from many sources, from the most devout chant to the worldliest folk tune.

Troubadour Melodies

Modern realizations of the medieval monophonic song literature revolve around the same bugaboos encountered in liturgical drama: rhythm and instrumental participation. The manuscripts are notated in the manner of contemporary chant, clear as to pitch but with no indication of rhythm or instrumentation.

To really grasp these problems we must consider the role of the courtly monophonic song literature. Often the poetry of monophonic song has been worked out with extreme care. A poet who takes so much trouble over his language would understandably not wish music to usurp his literary creation. Thus we find that relatively uncomplicated melodies are typical of these songs, and little attempt is made to provide any sort of word painting or other direct relationships between music and text. The obvious conclusion is that, just as with chant, the troubadours conceived music to serve the word, and to enhance but not overpower their poetry.

Also like chant, most monophonic songs survive in sources notated long after the creation of the work itself. These manuscripts do not start appearing until the 13th century, over 100 years after the beginning of the troubadour movement. Unlike chant, however, troubadour melodies vary widely from manuscript to manuscript. Further, in many collections (especially those of the troubadour repertoire) only a small proportion of the poems were provided with music. The extremes of the variations indicate that the melodic form was less fixed than the poetry. It suggests that the performer of courtly monodic song was allowed great scope and spontaneity in realizing the melodies—precisely the opposite of the situation with chant. Today's performer might bear in mind this spontaneous aspect of troubadour melody, and regard notated versions which have come down to us more like sketches which must be fleshed out in performance than like inalterable scores.

Rhythm

Now the problem of rhythm should make more sense. The main issue revolves around whether the rhythm of the songs should conform to a musical tradition apart from the texts, such as the modal rhythm of 12th-century polyphony (regular patterns of precisely measured longs and shorts; see Chapter 4), or whether it is based upon the rhythm of the words. The latter option offers no real solution since the rhythm of the poetry is highly controversial. Curt Sachs offers some straightforward reasoning: ''The use of a rhythmically noncommittal notation in times when a metrical script was available indicates a free or optionable rhythm.''

At the present state of knowledge the best advice to the performer seems to be to let the poetry dictate the rhythmic style. Hendrick van der Werf, one of the foremost authorities on troubadour music, remarks: ''By presenting the melody of a chanson as rigidly as our notational system requires, one risks directing too much attention towards the melody, and one may well obscure one of the most important characteristics of a chanson: it is a poem performed to a simple and unobtrusive melody in such a way that the text receives the almost undivided attention of performer and listener alike.''

Instrumental Accompaniment

The assumption prevails that troubadours generally sang to instrumental accompaniment, and, moreover, that this accompaniment was often of an elaborate and lavish nature. In fact, a survey of medieval narrative literature, song texts, and iconography turns up very few unambiguous references to a singer accompanying himself or being accompanied by other musicians. Undoubtedly the performer was free to realize the music with or without accompaniment as suited the occasion and available resources.

What kinds of instruments did the troubadours use? One scholar of troubadour and trouvère practice, Maria Fowler, has ascertained that vielles (fiddles) and small harps were far and away the most often mentioned instruments in the context of song accompaniment. This does not mean that other instruments were never used—we know better [see Chapter 3]—but does suggest discretion in modern recreations. Even more restraint should be applied in choosing the size of the accompanimental forces. The number of instruments described or illustrated rarely exceeds two (and these were generally relatively quiet instruments, better suited to indoor than outdoor performance). No evidence is available to confirm the presence of large groups such as frequently appear in the recordings of this repertoire. Modern performers seem to be confusing practices suitable for popular entertainment with those intended for an elitist art.

Once the feasibility of instrumental accompaniment is granted there remains the question of its role. Several possibilities come to mind. The instruments could simply supply drones on the central tones of a melody. Preludes, interludes, and postludes based on the melodic material could be devised. The instrumentalist might double the melody of the vocalist, or he might take this a step further by adding bits of ornamentation (heterophony). He might even invent an accompaniment which, while deriving from the vocal line, attains an independent life of its own. Any or all of these possibilities could exist in the same performance. And of course a song might be accompanied by a single person or by a group of players. As we shall see shortly in the discussion of the recordings, the current trend is to elevate the role of instruments to a status equal to or even surpassing that of the singer. This may have something to do with the background of the performers: most early music groups were founded by instrumentalists.

The Voice

It is difficult to have any definite picture of what vocal quality the troubadours strove to achieve. Strength, clarity, and sweetness are those attributes contemporaries most frequently admired. This really tells us very little. Strength, for example, may be taken to represent power and loudness, or it might refer to confidence and sureness of manner. Clarity might allude to a focused tone, or to precise articulation. One era's conception of beauty can be quite dissimilar to another's.

SELECTED RECORDINGS

Liturgical Drama

THE PLAY OF DANIEL
New York Pro Musica; Noah Greenberg, director
MCA 2504
THE PLAY OF HEROD
Pro Cantione Antiqua of London; Edgar Fleet, director
Peters International PLE-114
FOUR SAINT NICOLAS PLAYS: FILIUS GETRONIS (The Son of Getron); **Tres Filiae** (The Three Daughters); **Iconia Sancti Nicolai** (The Icon of St. Nicolas); **Tres Clerici** (The Three Students)
New York Ensemble for Early Music; Frederick Renz, director
Musical Heritage Society MHS 824437 or Music Masters 20049/50 (two discs)
LUDI SANCTI NICOLAI (The Miracles of St. Nicolas). Includes two of the St. Nicolas plays: **Tres Filiae** and **Iconia Sancti Nicolai**
Studio der Frühen Musik; Thomas Binkley, director.
EMI Reflexe 1C 065-30-940

For the modern listener, probably the most captivating of all liturgical dramas is *The Play of Daniel*. Its powerful story and musical richness (there are some 50 unique melodies) always make an impact. Fortunately, its first recording, the granddaddy of liturgical drama records, remains fabulously vital and entertaining. The New York Pro Musica's famous 1958 disc has the group's founder and director, Noah Greenberg, taking the spectacle route: his rendition fairly bursts with pageantry, rhythmic excitement, and instrumental color.

The Pro Cantione Antiqua's version of two conflated 12th-century Herod plays entirely dispenses with instruments, and, moreover, refrains from metricizing the music—with a single (and hence all the more effective) exception. All the singers are male. Perhaps the only controversial aspect of their realization is the occasional "improvisation" of simple counterpoint against the chant melodies. Another novel feature, also found in the group's chant performances on the reverse side (see the recordings discussion in Chapter 1), is the pronunciation of *c* before *e* or *i* as *s*, not *ch*, in accordance with medieval practice. So much for specifics. This is a flexible, fast-paced interpretation that is beautifully sung, very nicely recorded (in an extremely resonant chapel, with careful attention to spatial effects), and is altogether compelling. It proves that orchestration is not a prerequisite for holding one's attention.

Somewhere between the spareness of the Pro Cantione Antiqua and the all-stops-pulled luxuriance of the New York Pro Musica lies Frederick Renz's album devoted to the four Saint Nicolas plays from a 12th-century Fleury manuscript. Renz accompanies his singers with a modest instrumental contingent, but those instrumentalists are often put to more than modest use, what with preludes, interludes, postludes, drones, and heterophony, as well as occasional flourishes and sporadic percussion punctuations. Particularly striking are the whining string effects used in *Iconia Sancti Nicolai* to underscore the Jew's distress at discovering the loss of his treasure. Most of the music is sung to instrumental accompaniment of one kind or another, as if Renz did not trust his singers with their unadorned melodies. Yet this instrumental background rarely becomes obtrusive, and the reconstructions are on the whole imaginative and communicative.

Although we live in an age of increasing depersonalization, musical and otherwise, somehow many early music groups manage to develop strong and distinctive personalities. One of the most distinctive is Thomas Binkley's Early Music Quartet (also called Studio der Frühen Musik). Consider their recording of two of the St. Nicolas plays. Binkley contends in his jacket notes (on what grounds I am not clear) that these plays should not be construed as Church dramas, but rather along the lines of entertainment at a county fair. Instruments, he feels, should interpret and reinforce the texts. Thus in *Iconia* he treats instruments as symbolic, with a *chitarya Sarasenica* (better known as *guitarra morisca,* a plucked instrument similar to the long-necked lute of the Near East) supporting the Jew versus a rebec (a fretless bowed three-string instrument of Islamic origin) for the three robbers. Like Renz, Binkley employs a continuous instrumental background. Unlike Renz, he is not satisfied with occasional heterophony around a basic drone, but calls for improvisatory string parts which sinuously intertwine around the voices. These string improvisations amount to a quiet jam session in which the vocal melodies (themselves very freely interpreted) serve as the point of departure. Binkley makes much of the possible Eastern influence on monophonic music. Indeed, his rendition of *Tres filiae* projects virtually no feeling of Gregorian chant as we understand it today. The result is mesmeric and convincing on its own terms, but its relation to known practice seems arbitrary in the extreme.

MUSIC OF THE MIDDLE AGES
Early Music Quartet; Thomas Binkley, director
Telefunken Das Alte Werk 6.35412 (four discs)
Includes *Chansons der Troubadours;* (6.41126); *Chansons der Trouvères* (6.41275); *Minnesang und Spruchdichtung* (6.41208); plus *Music of the Minstrels, Telefunken Das Alte Werk 6.41928* [see Chapter 3]

PLANCTUS. Spanish and Troubadour laments
Studio der Frühen Musik; Thomas Binkley, director
EMI Reflexe 1C 063-30 129

CAMINO DE SANTIAGO I/II: MEDIEVAL MUSIC ALONG THE PILGRIM ROUTE OF SAINT JAMES, 13TH CENTURY
Studio der Frühen Musik; Thomas Binkley, director
EMI Reflexe 1C 063-30107/8 (two discs)

MARTIN CODAX: CANCIONES DE AMIGO (7); BERNARD DE
VENTADORN: CHANSONS D'AMOUR (2)
Studio der Frühen Musik; Thomas Binkley, director
EMI Reflexe 1C 063-30 118

Binkley's theories are nonetheless worth careful scrutiny, for his
Early Music Quartet has specialized in the secular monophonic
repertoire to a greater extent than any group on record. Without
exception their recordings are stimulating and accomplished, and
grow increasingly experimental. This development may be
clearly traced by comparing their Telefunken discs, most from
the 1960s, with their Reflexe albums, all from the last decade.
Vocal production becomes bolder, declamation more spontaneous. But at least the singers have a text and melody to restrain
their wildest impulses. The EMQ instrumentalists, with no music
to call their own, have developed astonishing expertise in the art
of improvisation, to the extent that their contributions go far
beyond mere "accompaniment" (as in *Tres filiae*). Binkley
justifies such extravagances this way: "A virtuoso instrumentalist would not be satisfied simply to play a drone, nor would the
poet-employer be likely to pay good money for inconsequential
services." Very true, but neither would the poet wish instruments to detract from the words of his poem.

Equally extravagant is the importance Binkley places on the
influence of Islamic culture upon European music from the 10th
to the 13th centuries and beyond. Binkley rightly argues that
during the numerous Crusades to recover the Holy Land from
Islam, Western musicians became thoroughly acquainted with
Islamic instruments, music, and musicians. Consequently, there
is good reason to assume that Eastern practice would affect
Western. And so many of the Early Music Quartet's recordings,
beginning in the mid-sixties with their historic *Carmina Burana*
album, are permeated with an Arabian flavor—one which becomes increasingly pervasive and persistent. Certainly the presence of Arab musicians and instruments in Europe was very real,
particularly in the Spanish peninsula. But presence hardly implies
domination. And all attempts to definitively document Eastern
influence on the surviving monophonic song literature have so far
failed.

Carmina Burana

CARMINA BURANA, Vol. I and II
Early Music Quartet of Munich; Thomas Binkley, director
*Telefunken Das Alte Werk 6.35319 (two discs, available separately as
6.41184 and 6.41235)*
CARMINA BURANA, Vol. I–V
Clemencic Consort; René Clemencic, director
*Harmonia Mundi HM 335/9 (five discs). Vol. I–IV also available as
Musical Heritage Society MHS 3471/3550/3666/3793*

The *Carmina Burana* is an excellent example of how an international monophonic repertoire was bound to regional performance
styles. Concordances for *Carmina Burana* songs may be found
in England, France, Germany, Italy, and Spain. The EMQ's
Carmina Burana discs attempt to capture regional differences in
performance styles.

The essence of Clemencic's approach may be gleaned from his description of the *goliards:* "Their faithlessness led them into a shadow-world that involved carousing, feasting, gambling, sloth, and prostitution." Though his ideas are wild and contrived, Clemencic never fails to beguile. His most interesting volume is No. 3, which includes the Gambler's Mass, a hilarious parody of a Mass proper. Since Clemencic's monophonic realizations tend to emerge as travesties of all we know about medieval performance practice, his hamming works perfectly here.

SECULAR MUSIC CIRCA 1300
Early Music Quartet; Thomas Binkley, director
Telefunken Das Alte Werk SAWT 9504

For an excellent sampling of the monophonic literature I would seek out the Early Music Quartet's anthology *Secular Music circa 1300*. It includes a pair each of the trouvère and minnesinger songs, one English song, two instrumental pieces, six polyphonic motets, ten pieces from the *Llibre Vermell*, an anonymous collection of non-liturgical sacred music, and Adam de la Halle's *Robin et Marion* replete with a healthy chunk of the spoken dialogue. The EMQ generates tremendous vitality—who says monophony has to be dull?

TROUBADOURS, Vol. I-III
Clemencic Consort; René Clemencic, director
Harmonia Mundi HM 396-98 (three discs)
MUSIC OF THE CRUSADES: SONGS OF LOVE AND WAR
Early Music Consort of London; David Munrow, director
Argo ZRG 673
FRENCH COURT MUSIC
Musica Reservata of London; John Beckett, conductor
L'Oiseau Lyre SOL-R332

Fascinating contrasts of performance style may be heard in the listed albums of troubadour/trouvère repertoire directed by Munrow, Clemencic, and Beckett. Beckett's Musica Reservata has cultivated a harsh, nasal approach to both vocal and instrumental tone production. The results are often raucous, but always invigorating—though best taken in small doses. Clemencic, more than any other performer of this music, has inspired among listeners equal amounts of devotion and distaste. With considerable panache his group merges the arabicisms of the EMQ with the shrillness of the Musica Reservata, throwing in a sizable amount of their own raunchiness. His second troubadour volume includes a chanson by the most famous of women troubadours, the Countess of Die. Munrow and his Early Music Consort represent an attractive compromise. Their performances are brilliant, lively, and at times moving. While they apply virtually all the styles mentioned in the course of this discussion, they manage to steer clear of overemphasis of any one: Eastern influence does not dominate, the instruments do not overwhelm the text, vocal tone never veers into the realm of the ugly.

Particularly instructive is a comparison of realizations of Raimbault de Vaquieras's (c. 1150-1207) *Kalenda maya,* one of the most frequently recorded of all troubadour songs, and one reportedly based on a dance Raimbault heard at the court of

Montferrat. Mezzo-soprano Jantina Noorman and the Musica Reservata, using just drums and a fiddle, give it a riotous, piercing, yet oddly satisfying interpretation. Noorman's peculiar tang must be heard to be believed. (This performance is also available on the Musica Reservata's *A Concert of Early Music,* Vanguard VSD 71223.) Clemencic precedes his version with a spoken *vida.* Vidas were short, often fanciful biographies of the troubadours found in 13th and 14th century manuscripts. The minstrels of the time evidently used them to set the stage for their performances. Clemencic underscores the recited vida with fragments of the *Kalenda maya* tune. His group's realization of the chanson reeks of ersatz Moroccan music. Binkley (on *Chansons der Troubadours;* 1970) performs *Kalenda maya* with a solo tenor and two fiddle players, spinning out the involved improvisations that are the hallmark of the EMQ. One telling aspect of Binkley's and Clemencic's practice here and elsewhere is their inclusion of the entire song. This generosity allows the poem to be viewed whole. It also represents a challenge to the singer and instrumentalists: what do we do when the music is repeated in the next stanza? Both Binkley and Clemencic adopt the correct attitude, I think: the music is not simply repeated verbatim, but varied in some way so as to give a sense of evolution.

HISTORY OF EUROPEAN MUSIC. PART I: MUSIC OF THE EARLY MIDDLE AGES

Soloists and Instrumentalists; Schola Cantorum Londoniensis; Edgar Fleet, director. Entire project under the direction of Denis Stevens also available as Harmonia Mundi HM 441-43
Musical Heritage Society Orpheus 349/51 (three discs, available separately)

As a welcome alternative to the instrumental excesses of the above groups, try the first two albums in Denis Stevens's History of European Music project. This series, which to the best of my knowledge never got further than the three discs listed above, was intended as a musical supplement to the scores in the invaluable Harvard Anthology of Music (see Chapter 4 for a fuller discussion). Most of the soloists stem from that brilliant corps of British singers whose names constantly crop up in what seems to be nearly every British early music album. Side 1 of the first disc is devoted to chant performed according to a variety of rhythmic theories, while side 2 of the second disc and most of the third disc focus on early polyphony. Side 2 of the first album contains troubadour and trouvère songs; and side 1 of the second album includes songs of the trouvères and minnesingers as well as examples of cantiga, lauda, and English medieval song.

These two latter sides fill several admirable roles. They permit a wide sampling of the medieval secular monophonic repertoire, choosing pieces that are readily available in a single volume for those readers who wish to follow along with the music. All the songs are sung unaccompanied, so that the listener can judge for himself whether or not instrumental accompaniment is as essential as some artists would have one believe. A variety of soloists are used, so that one never tires of the same vocal timbre. And the singing itself is both technically accomplished and musically convincing. The performances are neither stiff nor gimmicky, but straightforward and expressive. *Kalenda maya,* for instance, gets treated not as a virtuoso exercise, but simply as the unpretentious tune it is. Guiraut de Bornelh's *alba* (dawn song) *Reis glorios* is presented in three different rhythmic transcriptions, so that the listener can vividly hear how radically the character of a melody can be altered just by changing its rhythm. In my estimation these albums provide an ideal introduction to secular monophony.

Las Cantigas de Santa María

CANTIGAS DE SANTA MARIA
Esther Lamandier, voice, harp, portative organ, and vielle
Astrée AS 59
LAS CANTIGAS DE SANTA MARIA
The Waverly Consort; Michael Jaffee, director
Vanguard VSD 71175

Cantigas is a generic term applied to the religious and secular poems of the Galician-Portuguese literature; invariably they were written in Galician, the poetic language of 13th-century Spain. As with most of the medieval secular monophonic repertoire, they are generally strophic songs, songs whose melody is repeated with each verse, like familiar Christmas carols. Most of the cantigas also included a refrain before and after each verse. Because of their clear formal structure and strong rhythmic shape (this is the only major body of monophonic song to be written in mensural notation), many of the tunes have a dancelike character and may well have been danced to on occasion. Apart from six love songs by Martin Codax the only cantigas whose music has been preserved are those in the Santa María collection. This enormous compilation of more than 400 songs was put together under the supervision of King Alfonso X (1221-84) of Castile and Leon.

The Cantigas are arranged in groups of ten, nine relating miracles of the Virgin Mary followed by a tenth in her praise. Their stories were for the most part well known. Though pious in dedication and intention, the subject matter of these songs ranges from delicate and pious to the earthy and downright grisly. For instance: in one of the miracles, Holy Mary cures a cleric whose legs had turned backwards for having made underwear from an altar cloth he had stolen. In another, a nun makes ready to run off with the knight who seduced her; in still another a woman is so frustrated by the death of her husband that she fornicates with her son, then nine months later drops the inevitable offspring in the privy. Alfonso's collection served as music for the court rather than the Church and was intended for connoisseurs rather than for clerics. In fact, a number of the melodies in the Cantigas were familiar troubadour or trouvère tunes adapted to new, moralized texts. The range of melodies is great; many are either derived from chants or are chantlike, while others have a folk flavor. Curiously none have been positively identified as Spanish in origin. Jack Sage in *The New Grove* has observed that "Alfonso's court was clearly a haven for French, Islamic and Jewish culture and a natural refuge for troubadours fleeing from Provence in post-Albigensian times; more than 100 of the *Cantigas* refer to France, Italy, England and other countries abroad.... In general, the *Cantigas* bear witness to the wisdom of a king able to rise above national limits in the service of religion and art.''

Esther Lamandier's *Cantigas* is a very special disc. Like the EMQ's mezzo-soprano Andrea von Ramm, by whom she seems to be influenced, Lamandier produces a clear, highly malleable tone which she can manipulate with fantastic agility. Lamandier gives a good deal of attention to the individual nature of her material, vividly characterizing each song. All nine of her selections are presented complete. And unlike nearly every other performer of courtly monophony on record, she accompanies herself (on organetto, harp, and vielle, precisely those instruments most appropriate for this purpose). This of course limits the extent and complexity of instrumental participation. Thus, though Lamandier's preludes and interludes are often quite extended and elaborate, as soon as the texted part enters she must of necessity turn her principal attention to the voice. Her delivery is extremely flexible, at times declamatory, as if her overriding interest was the telling of a tale—which, at least in the case of these Cantigas, is exactly what she is doing. The result is eminently believable: we can well imagine that this is just how an accomplished minstrel might have executed these songs. And it is an agreeable respite from the instrumental excesses so often heard elsewhere.

As with the New York Pro Musica's liturgical drama recordings, the Waverly's *Cantigas* album stems from their live productions. A narrator relates in English the stories of eight of the miracles, while the two soloists (tenor Constantine Cassolas and the now celebrated mezzo Jan DeGaetani) are supported by a pleasing variety of instruments (some not medieval), all performed with enviable enthusiasm and polish. A purely instrumental number based on five of the cantigas serves as a long interlude—in the actual production this functioned as a marvelously effective intermission. Here, more than anywhere on this disc, the Consort goes all out to achieve Eastern effects—the use of a small clay drum imparts a flavor that is as much Indian as Arabic.

English

MEDIEVAL ENGLISH LYRICS
Assorted singers and instrumentalists. Frank Lloyd Harrison, music editor and director; Eric J. Dobson, poetry editor and director
Argo ZRG 5543

Without question the finest sampling of the pitifully small surviving corpus of medieval English song is that contained on the above Argo disc (see Chapter 5 for further commentary on this wonderful album). Not only are the performances outstandingly accomplished (among the singers are such well-known artists as Grayston Burgess and Gerald English), but considerable pains have been taken to render the songs in authentic Middle English. No words can convey how drastically this affects one's perception of the music, music that seemingly stands apart from the continental monody of France, Spain, and Germany in melodic style—differences better heard than described.

3

MEDIEVAL INSTRUMENTAL MUSIC

Hardly any medieval instruments survive. Eyewitness accounts of medieval music-making are not abundant, nor is there much to be found in the way of other written records. The number of medieval manuscripts containing genuine instrumental music may be counted on one's fingers. And while the practice of folk musicians in such places as Greece, Turkey, the Balkans, and the Middle East may supply vital insights into medieval performance practice, now is not then—subtle and not-so-subtle changes are inevitable over the span of centuries, no matter how isolated a culture might be.

Iconography of Instruments

In this era of photography, we are given to taking realistic-appearing art literally. When applied to art of the Middle Ages, this attitude can be perilous. Some medieval artists drew instruments without any knowledge of their workings. Others would picture groups of instruments with considerations of composition primary, accuracy secondary. A painter might choose not to show a wind player with puffed-out cheeks, preferring that his subjects look seemly. He may purposely portray mythological or fantastic subjects—Bosch and Bruegel immediately come to mind. Representations of musicians and their instruments might be deliberately satirical. A work of art might be symbolic or allegorical; angel concerts and depictions of King David are familiar instances. Numerological considerations might determine the number of instruments and musicians pictured.

Caveats aside, iconography can provide a wealth of information about not only the instruments themselves but also their place in society. Sizable ensembles were apparently the exception rather than the rule—medieval illustrations of single players or small groups far outnumber those of voluminous forces. Most of the big groups are found in depictions of a ceremonial or ecclesiastical nature.

Types of Instruments

Medieval ensembles of whatever size probably did not strive for the sort of studied refinement found in the great modern orchestras. In fact, more than musicians of any succeeding era, those of the Middle Ages valued distinctive and contrasting tone colors. Heterogeneity of sound—getting the most from the least—was the goal, not homogeneity. Thus while Renaissance musicians were inordinately fond of balanced groups such as a consort of recorders or krummhorns, in medieval times a quartet might consist of organetto, recorder, fiddle, and percussion.

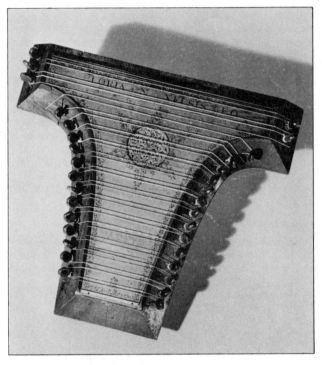

Psaltery, a plucked string instrument originating from the Near East and making its way to Europe during the Crusades.

Medieval instruments fall into two general categories: loud, or *haut* (brass, drums, and most winds) and soft, or *bas* (recorders, and most strings, including harps, psalteries, dulcimers, and lutes). The *haut* instruments were best suited for grand or outdoor functions, the *bas* instruments for indoor or intimate occasions. Usually the categories were not mixed, though percussion could be used with both. Brilliance was the byword. Even the *bas* instruments were brighter and louder than their Renaissance and baroque counterparts—damping mechanisms were seldom found on dulcimers, psalteries, harps, or harpsichords, and guitars and lutes were plucked not by hand, but by a plectrum of quill or horn. Most medieval instruments played in the treble range; dark colors were evidently not favored. Many were equipped with drones, among them bagpipes, fiddles, portative organs, double winds, and hurdy-gurdies. When circumstances permitted, percussion instruments were called upon to add sparkle and solidify the rhythm.

Relatively few of these instruments originated in Europe. Harps came from Syria, fiddles from the Balkans; guitars were Arabian, recorders Spanish; the trumpet was Saracen in derivation, the lute Moorish. Not until the late Middle Ages were these instruments transformed into something unmistakably European.

Instrumentalists

Who did the playing? Practically anyone who could buy or build an instrument. Though instruments were available to members of both sexes and to all social classes, not every instrument was available to just anyone. Trumpets and timpani, for instance, were associated with royalty and became their prerogative. Trumpeters and their attendant drummers consequently occupied the highest social position of all professional musicians; woe to those who played these instruments without official approval.

Of course professional musicians did not exist only to announce the presence of royalty, sound the call of battle, accompany their masters on long journeys, or provide the troubadours with a public outlet for their creations. Men and women would bathe together at the spas to the music of the minstrels. No important meal would be without instrumental accompaniment. Gaston Phebus, a 14th-century nobleman, described his ordinary day thus: "Hunting! after the hunt, Mass; after Mass, the womenfolk and the minstrels."

Jongleurs

Naturally music-making was not restricted to the wealthy classes. From the itinerant jongleurs, the common people learned the hit songs of the day, kept up with the latest news and gossip, and brushed up on their dance steps.

The jongleurs, who might be of either sex, served the function of newspapers, radio, records, movies, and TV, all rolled into one. They were everywhere: at weddings, tournaments, feasts of the rich and poor, vernacular plays, festivities and celebrations of every sort. Their presence did not require special occasions. They might be found plying their trade in the streets during the day, in the taverns at night. Where there were people there were jongleurs.

Jongleur translates as juggler. And indeed, many jongleurs were jugglers and much more besides. Their purpose was to entertain in every conceivable way; the more they could do, the more they would be sought out—and the more they would earn. Enormous musical versatility was expected.

Jongleurs inspired a curious mixture of delight and antipathy. The common people marvelled at their skills yet all the while feared these talents were gifts from Satan. The Church authorities, not surprisingly, hated them. They disliked their instruments, their often bawdy songs, their dances.

As Europe grew increasingly urban, the jongleurs established guilds and unions for the very same reasons musicians do today—to assure their rights, ensure employment, learn from one another, and preserve their skills and repertoire. Thus what was at first an essentially lonely and individual art grew into a protective and tightly-knit community.

Sources

Little instrumental music of the time survives. Performers for the most part learned tunes by ear and would pass them on the same way. The few pieces that do endure are basically of three types: dance music; keyboard music (especially arrangements of vocal works); and textless motets or *clausulae* [see Chapter 4] that some scholars feel were intended for instrumental realization. The most important repertoire of medieval instrumental music—though one still often related to vocal models—is dances. The chief sources of dances are two: *Le Manuscrit du Roi*, a late 13th-century *chansonnier* of trouvère songs in which eleven dances appear; and British Museum Ms. 29987, an early 14th-century Italian manuscript of secular polyphony which contains a grand total of 15 dances. All 26 dances are monophonic. Three polyphonic dances may be found among the six pieces in another manuscript, the Robertsbridge Codex, c. 1325, the earliest known collection of keyboard music.

Types of Dances

By far the most frequently named dance is that called *estampie*. It might also be spelled *instanpita, stampita,* or something similar. The word derives from the old Provençal verb *estampir*, meaning strike with the foot or simply to stamp. The estampie clearly is related to song, for it appears both as an independent instrumental piece and a poetic form. The only extant example of estampie poetry with music is *Kalenda maya* (see Chapter 2). All surviving instrumental estampies—indeed virtually all surviving medieval dance music—follow the same basic formal pattern. They are organized into a series of sections termed *puncta*. Each puncta is repeated, resulting in a general structure aa bb cc dd, etc. The first section would usually be open *(ouvert)*, ending with an incomplete cadence; the repeat would be closed *(clos)*, concluding with a full cadence. Thus the repeat was essential to complete the thought. In shorter, livelier dances such as the *salterello* and *trotto*, the initial puncta would often serve as a refrain.

Many dances are more complicated. Their succeeding puncta pairings are not based entirely on new material but rather derive melodic phrases and figurations from the initial tune. In *Lamento di Tristano* and *La Manfredina*, both from the British Museum's Italian manuscript, this principle amounts to a variation scheme. So sophisticated are some of the dances in this collection that they may well be the earliest examples of stylized dance—music intended for listening, not dancing. Many of these written-out dances were virtuoso pieces which, if executed at all, were danced by the adept. The 13th-century French music theorist Johannes de Grocheo pronounced the *stantipes* so difficult to dance that it "served to restrain the youths from wicked thoughts."

The Role of Instruments

We know what instruments were played in the Middle Ages, but the actual combinations of instruments are largely educated guesswork. Composers did not bother to indicate a specific ensemble instrumentation until the end of the 16th century. Instead, the music was expected to be adapted to the performing forces and the occasion at hand. Thus a monophonic dance at a peasant gathering might have been played by a lone fiddler with drone accompaniment. That same dance might have been played after a courtly banquet by a contingent of six and an instrumentation of twice that number (remember that most minstrels could play several instruments). The more skillful the performer, the more he would depart from a simple tune, fashioning it to the special qualities of his instrument.

We should be very careful to keep the role of instruments in their proper perspective. Up to the beginning of the 19th century (the time of Beethoven) art music was primarily vocal in emphasis: Mozart, for instance, viewed as his greatest and most important creations not his symphonies or concertos, but rather his operas. Almost all medieval instrumental music has its origins in vocal models. The same might be said of the instruments themselves. As late as 1535 we find the recorder and gamba virtuoso Sylvestro Ganassi, in his preface to the first recorder tutor, emphasizing: "Be it known that all musical instruments, in comparison to the human voice, are inferior. . . . For this reason, we should endeavor to learn from it and to imitate it."

If instruments reflected vocal models, then logically we should be able to deduce something about the nature of vocal production and practice from these instruments. For example, the seeming medieval preference for the simultaneous combination of different types of instruments is mirrored in their emphasis upon stratified vocal polyphony (see Chapters 4 and 5). Similarly, the relatively reedy, bright, and high-pitched character of medieval instruments undoubtedly found a counterpart in vocal timbres. Voices then very likely sounded far more Oriental than we tend to hear in modern-day recreations (consider the non-European origin of most Western instruments). And the impossibility of achieving a wide dynamic range on most medieval instruments suggests a similar restraint with respect to voices.

The essential message should be clear. Enjoy medieval instruments to the fullest, but do not elevate them to a position higher than the greatest of all instruments—the human voice.

SELECTED RECORDINGS

Introductions

INSTRUMENTS OF THE MIDDLE AGES AND RENAISSANCE

David Munrow and the Early Music Consort of London. Includes 98-page illustrated book by Munrow
Angel SBZ-3810 or EMI HMV SLS 988 (two discs)

There are not many albums devoted solely to medieval instrumental music. There is not much medieval instrumental music to record. Most selections from this repertoire may be found within medieval vocal collections or instrumental collections dominated by Renaissance music. The same pieces tend to appear again and again—wonderful if you wish to investigate the range of performance possibilities, less so if you wish to avoid duplications.

An ideal introduction to the instruments of the Middle Ages and Renaissance can be found on David Munrow's album of that title. Munrow and his Early Music Consort illustrate virtually all the major instruments with short examples drawn from medieval sources. Many of these examples are vocal in origin, but then vocal music was a primary source of instrumental material in the Middle Ages. Without exception the performances are vivid and persuasive; some are of astonishing virtuosity. That is not all. With this album comes Munrow's book of the same name, a book which has been sold independently for more than the price of the two-record set. This book is a tremendous accomplishment. With prose as lively and natural as his playing, Munrow writes what amounts to a social and political history as reflected in man's musical instruments. The information is up-to-date; scholarly footnotes are provided for those wishing to pursue the subject matter further, and the book is profusely illustrated.

Medieval Instrumental Music Anthologies

MUSIK DER SPIELLEUTE (Music of the Minstrels)
Early Music Quartet, Thomas Binkley, director
Telefunken Das Alte Werk 6.41928
ESTAMPIE (Instrumental Music of the Middle Ages)
Studio der Frühen Musik and Schola Cantorum Bariliensis; Thomas Binkley, director
EMI Reflexe 1C 063-30 122

These two albums contain minimal duplication. *Estampie* draws its contents entirely from the British Museum's Italian manuscript; *Music of the Minstrels* draws from several sources, though the two pieces from the Robertsbridge Codex are played not on keyboards, but by pairs of lutes and fiddles, respectively. As with his monophonic song recordings, Binkley's realizations here are wildly imaginative and expertly played, and rich in improvisation and Arabic color. But in the end they are not very satisfying. The *Estampie* album in particular relies too much on a good thing: virtually every dance follows the pattern of a slow, rhapsodic start that gradually grows faster, busier, and more definite in beat. However well-intentioned, both Binkley recordings produce an ersatz effect, reminiscent more of Hollywood than of the Middle Ages.

Collections Including Medieval Instrumental Music

MEDIEVAL MUSIC (The Jolly Minstrels: Minstrel Tunes, Songs, and Dances of the Middle Ages)
The Jaye Consort with Gerald English, tenor
Pye Golden Guinea Collectors Series GSGC 14092, Vanguard Cardinal VCS 10049, or Everest 3447
TANZMUSIK DER RENAISSANCE (Dance Music of the Renaissance)
Ulsamer Collegium; Josef Ulsamer, director. With Konrad Ragossnig, lute and guitar
DG Archiv 2533-111
MUSIC FROM THE TIME OF BOCCACCIO'S 'DECAMERON'
Musica Reservata, conducted by John Beckett
Philips 802 904

Music of the Hundred Years' War
Musica Reservata, conducted by John Beckett
Philips 839 753
Music of the Gothic Era
David Munrow and the Early Music Consort of London
DG Archiv 2723-045 (three discs)

The Jaye Consort's album was first released in 1967. Unlike many of its contemporaries, it has weathered the intervening years very well. Included are 25 medieval numbers of wide-ranging nature, of which 15 are purely instrumental. More than 15 different instruments are employed at one point or another, but with welcome reserve. The group never allows novelty of sound to override musical sensibility.

Strikingly creative are the performances of five dances from the British Museum Italian collection by the Ulsamer Consort on their largely Renaissance album. The familiar *Lamento di Tristano* receives a persuasively sinuous interpretation suggesting a harem setting; the *Istampita Ghaetta* features a drum part of jazzlike intricacy; the *Trotto* is given a lusty rendition on solo fiddle with drone. Also notable are the seven instrumental numbers found on the Musica Reservata's *Decameron* collection, with playing that is piquant and compelling in the group's best primal manner. Their collection *Music of the Hundred Years' War* is equally good, containing four organ pieces among its seven instrumental selections.

Many delightful things turn up in strange places. Among the New York Pro Musica's vocal albums often may be found instrumental gems. David Munrow's magnificent *Music of the Gothic Era* (discussed further in the next chapter) contains seven untexted motets from the Bamberg Codex (c. 1260) believed to be the earliest non-dance music intended for instruments, and here so realized. Especially fascinating is the use of *hocket* (hiccup), the division of a melodic line between different instruments (or voices, as the case may be) so as to produce a hiccup effect. Munrow's realizations are colorful in the extreme.

4

THE
RISE
OF
POLYPHONY

Not all medieval music was monophonic. On the face of it this statement sounds quite obvious, yet today's commonplace was in the Middle Ages a revolutionary step—the development of genuine polyphony. Polyphony may be loosely defined as music with two or more different yet related melodic parts. The systematic development of part-writing, and the harmonic vocabulary that must of necessity accompany it, distinguishes Western music from that of every other culture, from the simplest to the most sophisticated.

Why Polyphony?
There are various explanations for how and why polyphony came about, all relying in part on the element of chance. Harmonies would inevitably occur during intentional heterophonic embellishment of a given melody; harmonies might also accidentally arise when two or more performers unintentionally diverged from one another during unison singing of a tune. In either instance, if the result was pleasing, it would doubtless be retained in future performances. This is one possible explanation for the chanting in fourths, fifths, and other intervals found in many societies, primitive and otherwise, and for the emergence of polyphony in general.

Why the West?
Any of the foregoing theories could just as easily apply to the East as to the West. Why, then, did Eastern cultures continue on their monophonic ways while the West focused on polyphony? The answer boils down to a single factor, the development of notation.

Music in all known cultures—ancient or modern, Eastern or Western—begins as an oral tradition (as, indeed, does any language). Whether in the sacred or secular sphere, music comes down from teacher to pupil. In any oral tradition change is inevitable over the generations; few people possess phonographic memories. Such change can be desirable: it allows a song or a text to be shaped anew as befits the time and purpose. But precise documentation also has its value, even at times a political purpose.

We noted in Chapter 1 that Charlemagne, in a stroke of brilliance, saw that exact preservation of chant melodies could serve the politically expedient function of helping to unify his subjects. Clearly he had little hope for maintaining control of his far-flung empire if the nature of the liturgy in the dominant institution of his time, the Christian Church, differed substantially from country to country, town to town, and even church to church. The only practical solution was to choose one Christian branch to be the dominant one, and then to enforce the conversion of all the others. Charlemagne's choice was Gregorian, and the principal means of lasting enforcement was notation. Through notation, then, a chant tune and liturgical practice could be fixed, and a political order consolidated.

What does all this have to do with polyphony? Simply this. While a single monophonic line of great complexity can be executed from memory by trained choirs, part-singing presents unique problems. One cannot arbitrarily take a group of melodies, sing them simultaneously, and expect an outcome as beautiful as the individual tunes. Try it. The inevitably disastrous consequence owes to a basic law of harmony: not all combinations of notes are equally attractive. Conventions of what is "harmonious" vary, but there are always constraints upon what is acceptable within any particular culture. In order to combine melodies, then, careful planning is necessary. And the most efficient way to achieve such planning is through notation.

There is still another problem with polyphony. Not only must the harmonies be planned, but in order to be planned effectively, each part must enter at the right time. This necessitates exact notation not only of pitch but of rhythm as well. Rhythmic notation, discussed in Chapters 1 and 2, was not a great concern of chant or troubadour composers, and in fact there was no reason it should have been. Many, perhaps most, of these melodies fitted their texts better when performed in a flexible rhythm, one easily achieved by a soloist or through the "conducting" of the choir praecentor. That brings us to a fundamental rule of notation (and of life): necessity prompts invention.

Parallel Organum

The first notated examples of polyphony consist of nothing more than chants (or, more precisely, chant excerpts) sung in octaves, fifths, and fourths. These appear in the anonymous late 9th century treatise *Musica enchiriadis* (Music manual) under the designation *organum,* a term whose etymology has yet to be satisfactorily deciphered. From the different contexts in which the word appears, it is apparent that organum was not new, but had been around (probably as an improvisational practice) for some time. Even for medieval composers, the musical interest of such parallel singing must have had its limits. In fact, a freer sort of polyphony may be found in the same treatise. Here the two parts begin at the unison, expand to the interval of a fourth or fifth, and then contract back to the unison. Thus the added part deviates from the chant in intervallic structure, and the composite result is a succession of different, rather than the same, intervals. Both categories commonly go under the designation parallel organum, as the latter is obviously a modified version of the former. Neither held much possibility for future development.

Independence of Two Melodic Parts

The organum found in the *Musica enchiriadis* and other treatises of the subsequent century were nearly all based on chants intended for choral realizaton. It follows that organum too was meant to be performed by the full choir. Such parallel organum, owing to its limited departures from the chant, could be readily improvised. As such, it did not need to be written down. And in truth it really wasn't—our examples come not from practical sources but didactic treatises.

By the time of the Winchester Troper (c. 1050), the largest source of 11th century organum, the situation had changed radically. The music of this troper is English in provenance, but probably French in origin. It is a revision of the first Winchester Troper (c. 980, source of the oldest musical version of the *Quem quaeretis* play, the earliest liturgical drama); 164 of the original chants are now set in two-part organum. But (insofar as we can tell from the largely staffless, poorly heightened neumes) a good bit of the part-writing in the added part does not move in parallel, similar, or oblique motion with respect to the chant, but rather in contrary motion. Sometimes the parts even cross one another. Thus the two lines begin to achieve genuine independence—the basis for true counterpoint and polyphony.

These trends intensified with time. A vivid testament is provided by the next great collection of polyphony, commonly designated St. Martial, since most of the sources were gathered together at the library of the Abbey of St. Martial in Limoges. Despite appearances, it is clear that the four manuscripts containing polyphonic works are not the product of a single monastery, but rather derive from locations throughout southwestern France (Aquitaine) and northern Spain. The St. Martial manuscripts represent the entire 12th century, perhaps even extending a few decades on either side. All told, there are 94 two-part pieces, most of these not based on established liturgical chants. Their liturgical function is thus uncertain—they may have served as unofficial additions to the liturgy or they may have played no part in the liturgy at all. Whatever their purpose, these pieces testify to the increasing freedom of the composer: many of the organa are based on preexisting melodies not drawn from liturgical chants, and an even greater number are apparently completely original both in text and melody.

The Florid Style

A further significant feature of the St. Martial organa involves a stylistic innovation. Up to now all organa had been written in note-against-note style, with one note in the newly composed part for every note of the chant, and moreover, one note for each syllable of text. The St. Martial composers extended this principle to neume-against-neume. Since a neume might contain from one to four notes, the basic note-against-note style could now encompass several notes against one, or even three against two or four against three. Such modifications would typically occur at the ends of poetic lines, as a sort of cadential embellishment. Indeed, the practice probably arose as a result of improvisation.

Extending this improvisatory procedure to its limits created a radically contrasting style. Each note of the lower voice was stretched out, and above it were placed long *melismas* of as many as 20 or more notes. A single piece of St. Martial organum would characteristically manifest both of these very different styles: the old style in which both parts moved in essentially the same time values, termed *discantus*, and the new florid (or melismatic) style, where a rapidly-moving upper voice was placed against a slow-moving foundation. The melismatic style predominates in the St. Martial repertoire, so much so that it receives the designation *organal*. Because of the long note values necessitated in the lower organal part, this part became known as the *tenor* (from *tenere*, "to hold out"). The upper part was called the *duplum*.

Very similar to the St. Martial works are 21 polyphonic pieces found in the Codex Calixtinus (c. 1170) from Santiago de Compostela in the northwestern Spanish province of Galicia. This is to be expected, for St. Martial was the final collecting point for the thousands of pilgrims who annually made their way to the shrine of the apostle St. James at the Cathedral of Santiago. The Compostela collection differs from the St. Martial repertoire primarily in that the bulk of its polyphony is built on responsorial chants—the way of the immediate future. The Codex Calixtinus also contains the first known example of three-part writing, the Benedicamus trope *Congaudeant Catholici* (Let Catholics Rejoice Together).

The Notre Dame School

Polyphony seems to have arisen spontaneously and independently among the churches within the Western Christian world. Many of these remained perfectly content with improvised polyphony. Among those churches developing a more sophisticated type of organum, no one center took the leadership. Toward the middle of the 12th century this began to change. Paris, which had become the cultural and intellectual capital of the West, now became the focal point for polyphony as well. Its musical preeminence may be attributed primarily to the work of one man, Leonin (fl. 1160–80), of whose life we know virtually nothing. We cannot even be sure that he worked at the Cathedral of Notre Dame in Paris, which was erected between the years 1163–1182 yet only came to be completed c. 1257. We do know that Notre Dame became the center for a polyphonic school bearing its name.

Leonin was recognized as the greatest composer of organum in his time. Apparently his efforts were primarily directed toward one huge work called the *Magnus liber organi* (Great Book of Organum). This book contains no arbitrary arrangement of pieces, but rather represents a concerted attempt to fit polyphony into the responsorial repertoire of the chief feasts of the entire ecclesiastical year. All these organa are in two parts and all are based on responsorial chants. The same basic styles found in the St. Martial and Compostela manuscripts are found here too: florid organal section juxtaposed against essentially note-against-note discant passages.

What makes Leonin's achievement so impressive is not merely its awe-inspiring scope or the beauty of individual pieces, but the music's total integration into the liturgy. "To enrich the divine service" was how Leonin envisioned his work. Responsorial chant, you remember, presupposes an alternation between a soloist and the full choir. Leonin's plan retains the choral portions of the chant, but for the solo portions substitutes polyphony. These polyphonic sections would be sung by soloists (anywhere from one to three to a part, depending on the importance of the feast and resources of the church). The tenor line of the polyphonic sections consists, note for note, of the corresponding solo section of the original chant. The syllabic-neumatic sections of that chant are set against a newly composed part in florid organal style, the melismatic portions against an upper part in discant style. This distinction came about as much for practical as musical reasons, for if each note in an already melismatic chant was provided with another melisma against it, the resulting piece would be interminable. As it was, Leonin's organa greatly extended the performance time taken by the original chant.

This process of expansion was continued by Leonin's equally mysterious successor in the Notre Dame circle, Perotin (fl. c. 1180–1225). Perotin's major concern was the revision of the *Magnus Liber*. He took Leonin's florid passages and replaced them with works in discant style (now the basis of the most up-to-date music). This served the dual purpose of modernizing these sections and of shortening their performance time. The latter concern seems not to have figured into Perotin's revisions of Leonin's discant passages, which are often enlarged to three, and in two instances, four parts, and which manifest considerably greater rhythmic complexity than their precursors. Sections of organa, in whatever style, were termed *clausulae;* replacements of the sort Perotin composed are often called substitute clausulae. Note that Perotin's revisions affected only the solo, polyphonic portions of the chant; he did not tamper with the choral, monophonic portions.

The Creation of Measured Rhythm

The accomplishments of Leonin and Perotin do not end here. Through their efforts and those of their contemporaries it for the first time became possible to look at a piece of music and immediately determine the exact rhythm in which it was performed. You will recall that chants, troubadour, and trouvère songs, and even early polyphony was notated in a manner that contained few clues toward rhythmic realization.

But as organum grew more and more complicated, methods of achieving exact alignment of the two or more simultaneous sounding parts became necessary. Otherwise objectionable harmonic and rhythmic clashes would ensue. Leonin provided a solution by introducing measured rhythm. Now the rhythmic progress of a piece was no longer dictated by the performers or choir director, but could be codified by the composer. The loss of freedom was compensated by the gain in precision. For the first time the composer could notate music with a steady beat, music one could actually tap one's foot to. This explains why much of Perotin's music in particular has a dancelike lilt.

The familiar term *plainchant* (or plainsong) comes to distinguish chant in its pristine state, without rhythmic indication, from chant which is given measured rhythm, *cantus mensuratus* (measured song). *Cantus firmus* refers to any melody—chant or otherwise—which serves as a basis for a polyphonic composition.

According to William Waite in his influential study *The Rhythm of Twelfth-Century Polyphony*, the foundations of measured rhythm derive from an ingenious application of St. Augustine's theories on poetic rhythm. Thus rhythms were organized into six patterns of long and short notes known as the rhythmic modes. These corresponded to the metrical feet of Latin verse. For instance: the first rhythmic mode is the pattern of long-short (the poetic trochee), the second mode short-long (the poetic iamb). Composers indicated the desired mode through specific successions of note groupings termed *ligatures*. But an endless succession of notes in the same relationship of long and short quickly grows tiring. Musicians overcame this dilemma by creating various ornamental neumes which allowed for modification of the basic rhythmic pattern.

Contrasting Qualities of Leonin and Perotin

Perotin carried Leonin's innovations several steps further. The duplum and tenor, previously restricted to the first and fifth modes, respectively, now incorporated all six rhythmic modes. These modes were moreover organized into larger structures of rhythmic/melodic motives. Such structuring appears most impressively in Perotin's three-part organa and his two magnificent four-part pieces, *Viderunt omnes* (written for Christmas 1198) and *Sederunt principes* (written for St. Stephen's Day, Dec. 26, 1199). Perotin's upper parts typically share motivic material, which gets distributed among the voices in varying degrees of rigidity, from loose imitation to voice exchange and even canon. Because the upper parts generally move in the same range, they cross continuously. By this means Perotin achieves a subtle exploitation of tone color as first one voice, then another assumes prominence. He intensifies this kaleidoscopic quality by overlapping phrases so that while one part rests others remain in motion. As a result his music has a powerful forward-driving momentum not evident in previous polyphony. In the discant clausulae of Leonin, on the other hand, both parts typically rest at the same time, creating a striking stop-and-go effect.

There is no reason to make judgements of inferiority or superiority between Leonin and Perotin; they are merely different. Leonin centers attention upon the upper voice, which pours out a profusion of melodic ideas in writing of wide range (characteristically an octave and a half) and brilliant figuration—his is true virtuoso solo music. On the other hand, Perotin, in expanding to three and four parts, thereby focuses less attention on any one, preferring to achieve an interdependence of terse motivic phrases among them. So greatly has Perotin enlarged his predecessor's time scale that a single word or even syllable of the chant tenor can usher in a new section of music. Since the rhythmic modes and patterns change from section to section, the total effect is one of enormous blocks of sound, where so simple a matter as the change from one vowel to another becomes positively cathartic.

Consonance and Dissonance

The new art of polyphony necessitated that composers consider not only successive but also simultaneous sound relationships. The harmonic, or vertical, aspect of music now demanded as much attention as the hitherto exclusively melodic, or horizontal, aspects. It did not take long to discover that simultaneously sounding intervals possessed distinctive characteristics. A second could not be mistaken for a third, or a fifth for a sixth. Thus arose the concepts of consonance and dissonance. Regino of Prüm (d. 915), in his *De Harmonica Institutione,* is perhaps the first to define these terms (and to employ the word organum in its harmonic sense). Those intervals "falling upon the ear pleasantly and uniformly" are called consonant, dissonant those "coming harshly to the ear." The medieval consonances were the unison, octave, fifth, and fourth, the dissonances the third, sixth, second, and seventh, These choices were hardly arbitrary. They reflected not only medieval taste but also the overtone series. Intervals derived from overtones closest to the fundamental possess the simplest mathematical proportion to that fundamental (the octave 2:1, the fifth 3:2, the fourth 4:3, but the third 81:64; reference to a good article on acoustics should clarify any confusion).

Since order was an important facet of the medieval mind, an ordered musical universe was essential. The medieval solution to consonance and dissonance was therefore logical and straightforward. Mathematically perfect intervals were regarded as consonant with one another; all others were imperfect and dissonant. Consonance was required on strong beats, but in between any degree of dissonance was tolerated. This system provides medieval music with its characteristic harmonic flavor, while at the same time posing difficulties for modern listeners accustomed to a harmonic language in which dissonances are more carefully prepared and resolved.

Conductus, Motet, Non-Liturgical Polyphony, and Notational Advances

The organa of Leonin and Perotin, no matter how elaborate, remained inextricably bound to a liturgical function. They were firmly based upon the chants which they replaced in the liturgy, and served to add special glory to the celebration of high feasts. But as organa grew increasingly long and complex, the original chant became more and more difficult to discern. When reduced to increasingly long, unmeasured note values in the tenor, this chant no longer served any melodic purpose. Change the notes and who would know it? Why, then, even bother to use a chant at all? Inevitably, therefore, composers tried their hand at music unrelated to chant—a development which has already been observed in the St. Martial manuscripts. And so came about the two most important genres of the 13th century, the *conductus* and the *motet.*

The chief distinction between polyphonic conductus and organum was the former's lack of dependence upon any preexisting material. Franco of Cologne (fl. 1250) described the technique: "Whoever wishes to write conductus should first invent the most beautiful melody that he can: then he should use it like a tenor in making discantus." Perotin was among the first to exploit this new genre.

Conducti serves as processional music; in the liturgy they would accompany a celebrant who needed to move from one place to another, and might also supply music for the filing out of clergy and congregation at the end of the service. Because of their processional nature, conducti had to possess a steady rhythm, and moreover, to maintain the same rhythm in all the parts. Thus they were always composed in discant style, with basically one note per syllable of text. Generally they were constructed in strophic verse form. The texts of conducti were, of course, original. "Around the beginning of the [13th] century," Albert Seay notes in his *Music in the Medieval World,* "Conductus became the cleric's way of commenting on the events of the day, the death of a king or bishop, the election of a pope, the accession of a king, or the seizure of a city in war." Eventually entirely secular pieces were written in conductus style.

But the most important secular genre was the motet. This, too, arose from liturgical concerns. All organa have but one text, that of the chant serving as the liturgical tenor. If melodic troping was permissible in polyphony, why not verbal troping as well? So the duplum was fitted with a text of its own, which was at first a paraphrase or glossing—in Latin—of the meaning of the chant text simultaneously being sung by the tenor. These polytextual pieces were called motets (from the French *mot,* signifying "word"). If the organum had three parts, then separate texts could be added for both the duplum and the highest part, called the triplum; if in four parts, then separate texts for all three upper voices. The former is called a double motet, the latter a triple motet. The added texts were glosses upon the chant.

Experiments grew bolder still. Why not eliminate the gloss character of the texts, and instead insert texts in the vernacular French? Why not get rid of the chant tenor entirely? All this happened, although at first it led to curious results. Some motets had polyglot texts with strange admixtures of the sacred and secular. A notable case in point is the early 13th-century motet *Quant voi-Virgo-Haec dies,* where the protagonist of the duplum sings a hymn of praise in Latin to the Virgin Mary while in the French triplum a lover pines for his sweetheart. Such a blending of the worldly and divine is typical of medieval thought. Polyglot motets soon proved the exception rather than the rule; and, needless to say, the church did not approve of them.

The upper classes quickly appropriated motets for themselves, and the new polyphonic genre replaced the monophony of the troubadours and trouvères as the preferred means of secular musical expression. The texts, however, were still focused upon love in all its aspects. Nor was the monophonic past rejected out of hand. Courtly or even popular tunes might serve as the tenor in a secular motet; they might even appear in the upper parts. Composers took delight in hiding familiar melodic material within the body of their work; connoisseurs reaped equal delight in discovering it.

Franconian and Petronian Rhythmic Notation

Modal rhythm permitted only six basic patterns; there was no means to notate the duration of a single note. Enter to the rescue Franco of Cologne, a music theorist. Franco contributed c. 1260 a notational system that was at once brilliant and—like so many strokes of genius—ludicrously simple. He replaced the ubiquitous square notes of the time with a series of variously shaped notes (and rests), each representing a specific duration. Franco's system is called *mensural*, after the title of his treatise, *Ars cantus mensurabilis* (The Art of Measurable Song). With it the restrictions imposed by the rhythmic modes largely disappeared. Yet Franco provided for subdivision of the individual notes into only two or three parts. This shortcoming was partially rectified around 1280 by the composer Petrus de Cruce (Pierre de la Croix) and his followers. With the aid of dots they subdivided the primary note value, the breve, into anywhere from two to nine semibreves. As a consequence of these rhythmic developments, Franconian and Petronian motets usually are structured in layers. The lowest voice moves in long note values, as was the case in the pre-Franconian era. The upper voices, however, no longer move at roughly the same rhythmic pace, but rather are now clearly distinguished from one another. In the Petronian motet in particular, this move upward from slow to fast, simple to complex, is the most conspicuous feature.

Music Achieves Primacy over the Word

The rise of polyphony wrought many changes. At this point it would be worthwhile to pause and consider their far-reaching consequences. Both in sacred and secular monophony music had served primarily to enhance the text. But when Leonin and Perotin spread out this text to the extent that the words lost their comprehensibility, then the text could no longer serve as the focus of attention. Similarly, the rhythm of both sacred and secular monophony is essentially the rhythm of the text. But the invention of modal rhythm permitted a musical rhythm independent of and even contrary to the prosody being set. Through the device of metaphor a poet could *suggest* several layers of meaning in a single line. But a musician could go him one better by setting this line in several concurrent layers, thereby making the metaphor *explicit*. The poet in turn could catch up by giving each musical line a separate text; these texts could comment on one another. This is just what happened in the motet. Yet even here the poet is limited by how many of these individual textual lines can be simultaneously absorbed by the listener—a factor largely determined by the composer's skill at differentiating between them. And so for the first time in history music reigned over the word. A texted piece might even be realized instrumentally without destroying its musical logic.

The threat to the Church that these developments posed should be obvious. Musicians, elated by their new powers, had no intention of reverting back to a secondary role. Clergymen were fearful that music's previously understood "higher goal" of praising God would deteriorate into self-serving sensuous beauty. As early as 1250 the Cistercians and Dominicans formally forbade polyphony in the service; they termed it a "disturbance." The criticism grew more and more vehement, and reached a head in 1324 in a bull issued by the Avignon Pope John XXII (1316–34).

Secular Uses for Polyphony

Only one 13th century composer of consequence is known to have cultivated polyphonic settings in secular forms: the trouvère Adam de la Halle. All 16 of his polyphonic songs were cast into molds which in the next century would stabilize into three fixed forms (about which more will be said in the next chapter): fourteen rondeaux, one ballade, and one virelai. These songs are all in three parts, and all were written in homorhythmic (essentially note-against-note) style with a single text, like the conductus. Thus Adam avoided the polytextual and rhythmic complexities of the motet, instead concentrating on an individual melodic style designed to reflect the sentiments of his poetry. His polyphonic songs admit two basic possibilities for perform-ance: all the parts can be sung, or any of the individual lines can be singled out for singing (the middle voice was generally the principal melody), while the others are given to instruments. Richard Hoppin, in his textbook *Medieval Music,* has suggested that Adam's polyphonic songs "may represent the first attempt to write down instrumental acompaniments that had hitherto been improvised."

A Change of Scenery: English Polyphony

The development of polyphony centered in and around France, and France provided the initial part-writing model for most other European countries. But in the 13th-century English church composers had begun to go their own way. They developed a harmonic language richer in thirds and sixths, and consequently fuller than that of their French counterparts. And the English placed great attention upon the compositional techniques of *rondellus* and *rota*. A rota is a round, a circle canon in which each singer takes up the same melody in turn in an endless cycle, thereby producing music in several parts. Rondellus is a modified version of this procedure in which all the parts enter simultane-ously at the beginning, but on a different phrase of the tune. Thus if the phrases of the first part are labelled abc, the second part would be bca, the third cab.

Sumer is icumen in (c. 1280), the most famous piece in the entire medieval repertoire, is an ingenious combination of rota and rondellus technique: the upper part is divided into twelve phrases, the lower part (called *pes*) into two. This pes is designed to be sung in rondellus style, providing a continuous ground. According to the manuscript, the upper parts were intended for realization as a rota in four parts. However, they are so con-structed that they can be performed in as many as twelve parts, and moreover, the entrances can be staggered in a number of ways. As many as fourteen different parts can therefore sound simultaneously! This astounding feat was achieved in a very simple way: the downbeats of the melody were limited to the pitches F-A-C, the upbeats to G-B-D, so that on strong beats there was a constant alternation of F and G triads. Passing dissonances were of no concern. The Sumer canon is the only piece in six (or more) parts before the 15th century and the only known example of the combination of rota and rondellus. Secular motets, incidentally, do not appear to have been cultivated in medieval England.

Performance Considerations

The modal notation of Notre Dame revolutionized rhythmic performance, because for the first time anyone, anywhere, who could read the notation could produce essentially identical results. Still, we must keep a sense of historical evolution, and remember that modal notation did not spring from a void. The earlier sources of the *Magnus Liber* are written in a manner far more ambiguous to read than the later ones. Undoubtedly this was reflected in the music-making: the original performances of Leonin's pieces were probably less regularly modal in rhythm than those in Perotin's time. Indeed, the earliest performances of the *Magnus Liber* organa probably displayed some sort of compromise between strict modal rhythm and freer chant per-fomance styles. Modal polyphony very possibly had its origins in actual practice. Pre-modal polyphony from the St. Martial/Compostela period (or even before), though in chant notation, very possibly was subjected to metricized rhythm. If so, Leonin merely devised a notational system to express what was already being done.

A New Role for Soloists

If organum arose from the parallel singing of chants by men and boys at different pitch levels, then polyphony might initially have been a choral practice. But by Leonin's time it was definitely soloistic—at least in Parisian circles. The very design of the *Magnus liber* tells as much, since only responsorial chants were used. The original choral portions remained so, while the original solo portions were expanded into polyphony, with the chant still present as the lowest voice. Thus there was a clear distinction between choral monophony and solo polyphony, a distinction which remained in effect at least until the early 15th century and probably much later. Remember too that the *Magnus liber* was conceived exclusively for high feast days. On such occasions it was customary to employ several soloists for the liturgical chants. Polyphony permitted them to sing together rather than successively.

The exact disposition of soloists in the Parisian repertoire remains unsolved. But thanks to recent scholarship, feasible solutions are more readily determined. The archives at Notre Dame document that during the 13th century no more than six singers were employed for polyphony on any given day; three or four made a more normal group. These soloists were drawn from the ranks of the chant choir (which at Notre Dame averaged 24 though it could reach as high as 100 on special feast days). For their special services they received approximately two to three times the pay of their less skilled colleagues. Since much of the Notre Dame repertoire calls for three or four voice parts, it seems logical to conclude that this polyphony was generally performed one to a part, with perhaps occasionally two to a part in the two-part pieces.

Further evidence for solo performance of Parisian polyphony appears in the manuscripts themselves. These are uniformly small in size, adequate for no more than a handful of performers at any given time. There is no reason to think that each singer would receive his own part (as is customary today), for surviving multiple copies are nowhere to be found, not surprisingly, since parchment was expensive and copying music time-consuming. Further, these cantor's books are limited exclusively to the polyphonic repertoire. They include only those portions of the chants set polyphonically; the complete chants must be found elsewhere.

The Place of Instruments

As more and more facts are amassed, the role of instruments in medieval and Renaissance vocal music appears more limited than previously thought. There is simply no reason to assume instrumental doubling in much of this repertoire; certainly it is not dictated by the needs of the music. In medieval Church music, organ and bells are theoretically permissible but circumstantially suspect. Edward Roesner, in the most notable recent study, states his findings: "I know of no evidence that an organ existed in Notre Dame in the 12th or 13th centuries or that such an instrument was ever used to accompany responsorial chant (and by extension Parisian organum) in the medieval service." That the organ would be suitable only for choral monophony is plain from the nature of the instruments themselves. At least until the late Middle Ages church organs were raucous in tone and awkward in action, so that their sound would overpower a small group and music requiring rapid motion was impossible to execute. Expressive phrasing was equally impracticable. Bells, like organs, were mainly reserved for hymns and sequences. There is no reason to suppose their presence in polyphony.

Improvisation

One of the major consequences of notation was that *composition* eventually replaced *improvisation* as the chief means of creating music, although improvisation of one sort or another continued to be practiced up through the Classical era. Medieval soloists singing monophony or polyphony were expected to add various sorts of extemporary flourishes and vocal colorations, as is amply attested by the theorists of the time. Such improvisation would naturally be most appropriate in rhapsodic styles such as the upper part of a melismatic organum. But even in stricter styles like the conductus, singers were counted upon to do more than simply read the notes off their part.

Tempo—A Matter of Sensibility

Brief mention must be given to the matter of tempo. Organum called for a tempo apposite to the festive occasion for which it was written. From the 10th-century Cologne treatise *De Organo* we learn: "Organum always requires a careful and deliberate tempo." Theorists distinguished between three different tempos for works in mensural notation: slow for those pieces in Petronian style, with many notes in the highest part; moderate for those pieces in Franconian style, with no more than three semibreves to the breve; and fast for pieces in hocket style. Times were changing.

SELECTED RECORDINGS

Contrary to accepted wisdom, instrumental additions to polyphony do not necessarily clarify the individual lines; what they *do* is detract from the singers and subtract from the expressivity, flexibility, tonal beauty, and nuances that only a human voice can achieve. Many older recordings fail in still another respect: they perform chorally what is soloistic music. This severely distorts the character of the music and greatly lessens its lucidity, for when additional voices are added to a given line the unique timbre of an individual voice largely disappears. The loss is particularly damaging in music with constantly overlapping upper parts, such as that of Perotin.

Anthologies

MEDIEVAL MUSIC: ARS ANTIQUA POLYPHONY
Pro Cantione Antiqua; Edgar Fleet, director
Peters International PLE 115

HISTORY OF EUROPEAN MUSIC, VOLUMES I–III
Schola Cantorum Londoniensis; Edgar Fleet, director. Denis Stevens, musical director
Musical Heritage Society Orpheus OR 349–51 (three discs, available separately). Also available as Harmonia Mundi HM 441–43

MUSIC OF THE GOTHIC ERA
The Early Music Consort of London under the supervision of David Munrow
DG Archiv 2723–045 (three discs)

ARS ANTIQUA: ORGANUM, MOTETTE, CONDUCTUS
Capella Antiqua of Munich directed by Konrad Ruhland
Telefunken Das Alte Werk SAWT 9530/31 (two discs)

Happily there is a recent album of early polyphony which dispenses with instruments and which for the most part opts for soloists where appropriate. I refer to the Pro Cantione of London's Ars Antiqua album, a sequel to their equally stunning chant/liturgical drama disc discussed in Chapters 1 and 2. Both are designed to accompany and illustrate examples in the excellent *Oxford Anthology of Music*. These examples cover virtually all the stylistic developments enumerated in this chapter, from parallel organum in the *Musica Enchiriadis* to complex Petronian motets. Despite their didactic intent, the performances are far from academic, and instead are full of enthusiasm and vitality without sacrificing polish. The singers produce a tone free of vibrato, one generally harsher and more penetrating than we are accustomed to, though by no means ugly in the Musica Reservata manner. Their distinctive vocal characters allow each line to stand out tellingly, and the realizations too are creative. For instance, the triplum is omitted the first time through the magnificent double motet *Caligo terrae/Virgo Maria*, an anonymous English work from the early 14th century. This not only introduces variety of texture, but allows the listener to more easily perceive the melodic beauty of the duplum and the highly embellished nature of the triplum.

Another, more extended overview of early polyphony is provided in the Harvard University Press *Historical Anthology of Music* (HAM), a boon to music students since its publication in

1946. While Harvard never saw fit to make their own recordings of the music in this anthology, substantial portions of it have been recorded on at least two labels, Pleiades and Musical Heritage Society. The Pleiades project, despite the best intentions and some informed participants, was ultimately crippled by the fact that the musicians are for the most part either ecclesiastics or students drawn from college collegiums. The singing and playing betrays all the usual amateurish flaws: imprecision, faulty intonation, unattractive timbral quality, lack of shaping on both the micro and macro levels. Simply put, the execution—with occasional exceptions—does not do justice to the purpose. Fortunately, the HAM recording under the supervision of Denis Stevens proves infinitely superior. Many of the singers are the same as in the Pro Cantione of London; Edgar Fleet is the superior director. While the performances are not up to the elevated level of those on the Pro Cantione's Peters disc (exhibiting such dubious practices as giving the lowest voice to an organ in some of the Notre Dame polyphony), they nonetheless are very good indeed. Moreover, there is no duplication between the HAM and Oxford Anthologies.

For more extensive concentration on the major sources and styles, it is necessary to turn to commercial anthologies; foremost among these is David Munrow's *Music of the Gothic Era*. Munrow's Early Music Consort presents some of the greatest works of Leonin and Perotin, including the latter's two stupendous four-part organa, *Viderunt omnes* and *Sederunt principes*, as well as a representative sampling of sacred and secular motets from the entire medieval period. The overlaps between this compendium and the HAM and Oxford anthologies are blessedly few. Like everything Munrow touches, the music-making is so sensitive, compelling, and just plain entertaining that criticisms seem superfluous. Though Munrow sometimes relies on editions that do not incorporate the latest research, he nonetheless bravely attempts to come to terms with what we do know of medieval performance practices. Examples: His group's execution of the ornamental note known as the *plica* observes the directions of the theorist Magister Lambert (c. 1240) who urged it be sung "with a partial closing of the epiglottis combined with a subtle repercussion of the throat." In the four *Magnus liber* selections, "two of the *duplum* parts have been assigned to counter tenors and two to tenors so that the listener may compare the use of 'normal' and 'falsetto' techniques." Similar strokes of imagination enliven the entire album. The only major reservation one might have concerns Munrow's pervasive use of instruments. Organ and/or bells are employed in all the Leonin/Perotin works, and every one of the 13th-century motets receives instrumental accompaniment of some sort.

Instruments prove even more problematic in Konrad Ruhland's 1968 Capella Antiqua anthology, which covers the same general ground as Munrow's (all Ruhland's selections, however, are sacred), but—in another happy circumstance—contains just one duplication. Ruhland displays far less restraint than Munrow in determining the size of his instrumental forces; moreover, he shows no qualms about rendering sacred music with instruments that would not have been allowed in any medieval church. Still, much worthwhile music and pleasurable

listening can be found here. Most valuable are the first two
bands, which contrast a two-part setting of *Pascha nostrum* from
Leonin's *Magnus Liber* with a later three-part setting in the style
of Perotin. The melismatic passages of the Leonin are rendered
in free rhythm, the organal passages in measured rhythm—an
effective and eminently believable procedure. If truth be told,
however, the Capella's music-making is too often tentative in
phrasing, sluggish in tempo, and amateurish in technique. Once
regarded as the last word, their performances have not weathered the test of time gracefully.

Specialist Collections

CAMINO DE SANTIAGO I/II: MEDIEVAL MUSIC ALONG THE PILGRIM ROUTE OF SAINT JAMES, 13TH CENTURY
Studio der Frühen Musik; Thomas Binkley, director
EMI Reflexe 1C 063-30107/8 (two discs, available seperately)

THE WORCESTER FRAGMENTS
Accademia Monteverdiana; Denis Stevens, director
Nonesuch H-71308

MUSIC IN HONOR OF ST. THOMAS OF CANTERBURY
Accademia Monteverdiana; Trinity Boys Choir; Denis Stevens,
director
Nonesuch H-71292

THE WORLD OF ADAM DE LA HALLE
The Cambridge Consort; Joel Cohen, director
Turnabout TV-S 34439
Includes 13 of Adam's polyphonic rondels, his *Robin et Marion,* and
some 11 assorted songs from the troubadour/trouvère literature

More selective repertoire appears in these remaining listings.
Binkley's two albums contain between them three pieces from
the Codex Calixtinus, including the famous *Congaudeant catholici*
on the first disc. The monophonic hymn *Dum pater* is graced with
Binkley's by-now-familiar elaborate instrumental heterophony,
and even includes improvised vocal organum at the refrain. The
two conducti, on the other hand, are rendered unaccompanied by
soloists. I find the results strikingly effective. As is their wont,
Binkley and his forces do not rely on preexistent editions, but
create their own versions, ones freer rhythmically than the
norm. As a consequence ornamental dissonances stand out
conspicuously. A provocative approach—and just as plausible as
more metricized realizations.

Denis Stevens restricts himself to English sources in his two
Nonesuch albums. One disc is limited to music from the Worcester Cathedral library, the other to works relating to St. Thomas à
Becket of Canterbury (1118–1170). Both include a wide range of
monophony and polyphony from the 12th through 14th centuries.
Not only are the pieces of uniformly high quality, but they have
been carefully grouped so as to effect a varied and attractive
sequence. And not only are the performances brilliant (some of
the soloists are the same as those in the Pro Cantione), but their
realizations are also extremely inventive. Consider the conductus *Novus miles sequitur* (1173) praising Becket. Stevens's
ensemble performs its outer verses in a three-part setting from a
French manuscript, the middle verse in a two-part setting from a
Spanish manuscript. Bells serve as accompaniment, but only as

punctuation—not as melodic instruments as on Munrow's anthology. Indeed, Stevens's handling of instruments in general is far more circumscribed, in line with recent research, than Munrow's. So splendid is the repertoire in these Nonesuch albums that I cannot resist mentioning two individual works: the irresistibly piquant motet *Thomas gemma/Thomas caesus* (c. 1300) leading off the St. Thomas disc, and the haunting 13th-century rondellus motet *Fulget caelestis curia* on the Worcester record.

Surprisingly, for such a famous piece, *Sumer is icumen in* has not fared well on disc. By far the most attractive recorded performance is to my mind that by a group of six outstanding British singers on *Medieval English Lyrics* (Argo ZRG 5443). Their unaccompanied rendition is made all the more effective by scrupulous attention to "authentic" medieval pronunciation. This wonderful album is discussed in more detail in Chapters 2 and 5.

Lastly comes the most complete single collection of Adam de la Halle's polyphonic music, Joel Cohen's Turnabout disc. These three-part pieces are attractively realized in a variety of ways: chorally, instrumentally, by unaccompanied soloists, as solos with instruments on the other two lines, but never, unfortunately, as solos with choral refrains. Though more polished and sophisticated performances of some of these pieces may be found elsewhere (including two on Munrow's Gothic Era anthology), Cohen's disc serves its purpose well. And it provides a good deal for the money: Adam's *Robin et Marion* is also included, as is a selection of 11 troubadour/trouvère songs.

5

THE 14TH CENTURY AND BEYOND

Good Times and Troubled Ones

The rapid rise of polyphony in the 12th and 13th centuries depended upon corresponding advances in style and notation. It was an age of head-over-heels invention. But once these innovations had been transformed into usable techniques, composers could concentrate on extracting the full potential of what had been learned. This process of consolidation and refinement was the task of the 14th century. Four major trends can be discerned; first, increasing secularization; second, the growing dominance of polyphony; third, the emergence of national idioms and forms; and fourth, an increasing preoccupation with musical technique.

Since music is a social art, it is altogether natural for musical trends to mirror the society producing them. The 12th and 13th centuries together formed a stable, unified period, one marked by relative peace and the central authority of the Church. Feudal society seemed to be working well, creating conditions that were ripe for the improvement of man's lot. The growth of trade, for instance, led to the appearance of great urban centers and the concurrent establishment of universities. Each of the three major social institutions enriched musical life: the castle courts supported the aristocratic art of the troubadours and the trouvères; the cathedral contributed the new art of polyphony; and the universities supplied a forum for the composers and theorists to disseminate their musical discoveries. No wonder so much happened so quickly.

Alas, this prosperity did not last long, for a combination of reasons. The institution of the papacy was in trouble, and in 1305 its site moved from Rome to Avignon for a variety of political reasons. This lengthy "Babylonian Captivity" (1305–1378) was followed by an even more troubled time, the so-called "Great Schism" (1378–1417), where there were two and for a time even three rival popes. Not until 1417 was the Church reunited at Rome under a single Pope. During this protracted period of religious confrontation, people lost faith in the Church's ability to cement society together. But things were hardly better in the secular sphere. Strife was the byword, both within and between countries. England and France embarked on a more than Hundred Years' War (1338–1453). The Black Death (1348–50) in just a few years decimated an estimated one-third to one-half of the population of Europe. All classes experienced discontent: the old feudal aristocracy was declining in the face of a rising bourgeois, and peasants wanted their say in the changing social order. A new age was at hand.

The Ars Nova

Two treatises appearing in France around 1320 provided a name for this age in music, Philippe de Vitry's *Ars Nova* (New Art) and *Ars novae musicae* (The Art of the New Music) by Jean de Muris. Modern scholars liked the term Ars Nova so much that they adopted it as a convenient catchphrase denoting 14th-century polyphony; by extension the polyphony of the preceding century (some expand it to include the Notre Dame school) became the Ars Antiqua. More specifically, Ars Nova refers to the music of 14th-century France; the Italian counterpart is dubbed the Trecento.

Either way, the novelty of the age was—at least in the eyes of the theorists—almost entirely a matter of notation. Even this is misleading, for no new notational system appeared, but rather refinements upon the now standard Franconian/Petronian mensural system. In this old system duple divisions of the beat (as in 2/4 or 3/4 meter), while feasible, were neither theoretically recognized nor adequately provided for, thanks to the long-standing mystical belief in the perfection of the number 3 (the Trinity, etc.). Until the 14th century ternary divisions (equivalent to our 6/8 or 9/8 meter) were the norm. The 14th-century theorists, interested more in practicality than in numerological mysticism, placed duple and triple mensuration on an equal footing. The smallest note of the old system, the *semibreve*, in theory capable of a wide range of time values, in practice was limited by the inescapable fact that all semibreves were identical in shape. Thus their values were completely dependent on context. It remained for new theorists like Vitry to modify the semibreve by giving it upward or downward tails turning it into an independent note value in its own right, dub it a *minim*, and allow it, too, to be divided into both threes and twos. The upshot was an enormous enlargement of rhythmic possibilities at every level. Whereas virtually all metricized music prior to 1300 can be transcribed in the equivalent of modern-day 6/8, Vitry's innovations permitted four distinct meters: 6/8, 9/8, 2/4, and 3/4. Moreover, these could even be combined simultaneously. Individual note values, too, could be notated with a precision and variety previously impossible.

Notational advances in the 14th century were but the means to an end: the triumph of polyphony. The principal musical action took place in the two mainstream countries, France and Italy, where old forms were revised and new ones invented to accommodate multipartite music. In France the chief novelties were the isorhythmic motet, the creation of polyphonic mass movements, and the extension of polyphony to such troubadour/trouvère forms as the ballade, virelai, rondeau, and lai. A new, entirely polyphonic form was devised—the strictly canonic *chace*. In Italy secularization was even more thorough. The Italians had their own equivalents of the virelai and the chace, the ballata and caccia, and a form all their own, the madrigal. In both countries the harmonic language grew increasingly refined. Without further ado, then, let us look at these developments in some detail.

Isorhythm

French music throughout history has been preoccupied with order, and in the 14th century the most notable manifestation of that concern was the principle of *isorhythm*. Its origins date back to the century before, when Perotin and his followers had noticed that to achieve the desired length in their substitute clausulae, the chant tenor had to be repeated. By organizing the notes into rhythmic patterns; they gave the tenor line shape, and increased the audibility of the chant. Musicians saw that two separate entities were at work: the rhythmic pattern, termed the *talea* (''cutting''), and the series of melodic intervals, termed the *color* (''repetition''). If sections of color and talea of different lengths are chosen, the patterns automatically overlap; each time they repeat, they coincide at different places. Moreover the notes of the talea might be augmented to double their length or diminished to halve it, to mention but two of the simpler possibilities. Nor did composers confine isorhythm to the tenor. As time went on, isorhythmic techniques began pervading the upper voices; typically, these voices would have their own rhythmic and/or melodic patterns.

The isorhythmic motet became the major art form of the French Ars Nova. Its appeal is easy to fathom. Isorhythm enabled the tight organization of extended works, no small advantage in pieces which can baffle all but the most informed listener with their surface complexity of polyrhythms, polymeters, and polytextuality. Isorhythm also satisfied the medieval penchant for abstraction and concealed meaning. Only the initiated could consciously discern what the composer had done, though even a casual listener could subconsciously sense some sort of underlying coherence.

The Roman de Fauvel

The earliest major source for isorhythmic motets is the *Roman de Fauvel*, a long poem by Gervais de Bus written in two parts, the first completed in 1310, the second in 1314. Gervais earned his living as a clerk in the chancellery of the kings of France from 1313 to 1338. His poem bitingly satirizes social corruption along the general model of the well-known tale of Reynard the Fox, versions of which date back to the late 12th century. The wily fox Renard is replaced by the conniving ass Fauvel. The very name Fauvel is full of hidden meanings. It is an anagram built from the initial letters of the vices Flatérie, Avarice, Vilanie (depravity), Variété (fickleness), Envie, and Lascheté (cowardice). Besides the word's derivation as an anagram, it also represents Fauvel's color, a dirty reddish-yellow (*fauve*), and his thinly veiled falsehood (Faux-vel).

Fauvel obviously struck a responsive chord, for the poem became enormously popular. All told, Gervais' poem was preserved in 12 manuscripts, though only one of these has music. This forms the first important collection of Ars Nova pieces. The extensive musical interpolations were chosen by Chaillou de Pesstain (c. 1316). *Fauvel*'s music dates from 1189 right up to 1316, most of it to Latin texts and most of it monophonic. From a purely historical point of view the thirty-four motets comprise the heart of the collection, forming as they do a contemporary anthology of the entire early history of the motet, from the early 13th century to the latest works of Philippe de Vitry.

Settings of the Mass Ordinary

The next important source of French Ars Nova music is a manuscript now residing in the Chapter Library at Ivrea. This Ivrea Codex was compiled c. 1360 around the environment of the papal court at Avignon. It includes some 80 pieces, many of them isorhythmic motets, including the later motets of Vitry. There are also a number of secular songs. But the most striking and unusual category is the 25 settings of movements from the Mass Ordinary.

For many centuries it had been customary to set the entire Mass to music. The lessons and orations would be recited by the priest, deacon, subdeacon, or other appropriate clerical figure, while everything else would be chanted by the schola or choir, perhaps also allowing for congregational participation. These chants conform to the basic portions of the Mass: the *Proper (Introit, Gradual, Alleluia, Offertory, Communion)*, which changed with each day, depending upon the particular season or feast, and the *Ordinary (Kyrie, Gloria, Credo, Sanctus, Agnus Dei*, sometimes also the dismissal *Ite missa est)*, which remained constant. (In practice the Ordinary too might change, thanks to tropes for specific occasions.) Though polyphonic settings of the Ordinary appear as early as the Winchester Troper (c. 1050), the first systematic use of liturgical polyphony was not until Leonin's *Magnus Liber* (c. 1160). Here polyphony provided showpieces in the Proper of the Mass for the soloists on the great feast days. After Perotin, hardly any liturgical polyphony was written until the Ivrea Codex and the subsequent Apt manuscript (c. 1385), both from the Avignon circle, where polyphonic settings of sections from the Ordinary begin to assume importance.

Most 14th-century polyphonic settings of the Ordinary are of single movements. Typically scribes grouped these movements by section in the manuscripts, so that five *Kyries* might be followed by seven *Glorias,* then six *Credos,* etc. The choirmaster could then select those movements best suited to the occasion. Once one or more movements of the Ordinary get performed polyphonically, polyphonic settings of the entire Ordinary become inevitable. That just such a practice gradually became accepted is clear from four Ordinary compilations, known today from the present location of their manuscript sources. These are the Masses of Tournai, Toulouse, Barcelona, and the Sorbonne.

But the greatest of the 14th-century polyphonic Mass Ordinaries, and the first to survive in a complete setting by one composer, is that by Guillaume de Machaut (c. 1300-c. 1377). It is Machaut's largest work and the best-known extended composition of the entire 14th century. While the anonymous settings are largely in three parts, Machaut employs four voice parts throughout. The *Kyrie, Sanctus, Agnus Dei,* and *Ite missa est* are all built upon chant tenors and are wholly or partially isorhythmic. The *Gloria* and *Credo* are given essentially syllabic, note-against-note settings; such a practice becomes increasingly customary, owing to the sheer length of the texts. What is unique about Machaut's setting of these two movements is the free strophic patterns into which they are organized. In fact, at one time Machaut's Mass was thought to be cyclic in the Renaissance sense that the movements were melodically related; this theory is now largely discredited. Nonetheless, its consistency of style, complexity, and thoroughgoing rhythmic organization suggest that it is a late work and one intended to be performed whole.

Guillaume de Machaut, Master of His Age

More than any other medieval musician, Guillaume de Machaut marks the end of one era and the beginning of another. He was the last representative of the trouvère tradition, yet the quintessential learned artist as well. He took holy orders at an early age, though he lived and worked almost entirely in courtly circles: like his most illustrious Ars Nova predecessor, Philippe de Vitry, Machaut was at once poet, composer, canon, and servant of kings. But unlike Vitry, who apparently devoted little time to artistic pursuits during the last 40 years of his life, Machaut miraculously managed to make the most out of all his careers.

Machaut lived more like a trouvère than a cleric, traveling widely with and for his patrons (perhaps as far as Poland and Lithuania) and writing his poetry and music on command for courtly occasions. This of course explains the paucity of religious music in his output. Machaut was equally esteemed as both poet and musician during his lifetime; in fact, three-quarters of his surviving work is unaccompanied poetry, full of structural intricacies and love for anagram and other riddles. His works were eagerly sought out by kings and nobles in France and elsewhere. The future king Charles V even paid him a visit at home in 1361. Near the end of his life Machaut supervised the compilation and arrangment of his total creative output (save five presumably very late works).

Up to the time of Machaut polyphonic music was generally what has been termed "constructive" in design. Composers wrote the music literally from the bottom up, with a chant or some other melody (preexistent or newly composed) serving as the foundation. Polyphony was number made audible: This abstract approach to music manifested itself in the mathematical basis of consonance and dissonance, in the isorhythmic principle, in the stratification of rhythmic layers, and in the multiple texts of motets.

But there existed another possibility: polyphony where melody, not rhythm, dominated. In monophonic music, which consists of just a single line, melody always dominates; but Machaut, like Adam de la Halle before him, enlarged trouvère monody to create polyphonic pieces which were in essence accompanied song. The expressive setting of a single text was still the foremost consideration; now, however, accompaniment parts were not improvised, but fully written out.

Machaut managed to concentrate on melody in his chansons by couching them in the standard *poetic* forms of the trouvères—namely *lais* and the three *forme fixes:* ballades, virelais, and rondeaux. Lais were narrative poems built in stanzas of variable structure. All Machaut's 20 surviving lais save four are entirely monophonic. One of those four, *Le lay de la fonteinne,* alternates monophonic stanzas with stanzas in three-part canon (chace); *Le lay de confort* is canonic throughout. Incidentally, Machaut notates both of these entirely as a single line; it is up to the performer to realize the canons.

Performed complete, Machaut's lais last well over 20 minutes. They do not depend on narrative interest alone to sustain the listener through this length, but create within their strict framework a small world of poetic, melodic, and rhythmic subtleties. Machaut's lais represent the pinnacle of trouvère composition in this form, an accomplishment so imposing that it inspired no successors.

Fixed Forms: Rondeau, Ballade, Virelai

Though superficially more progressive than the lais, Machaut's polyphonic songs in fixed forms in some respects actually maintain a closer tie to the past both poetically and musically. All three of the formes fixes probably originated as strophic dance songs with group refrains. They differ primarily in their repetition scheme. To simplify, let capital letters indicate refrains of text and music, lower-case letters melodic repetitions with new words but identical rhyme scheme. In this scheme, each stanza of the rondeau would have the form ABaAabAB. The *ballade* was fixed musically (aabC) but not poetically; its three stanzaic divisions would typically consist of a pair of couplets and a variable section, followed by a concluding refrain. Thus a seven-line stanza might look like this: ab-ab-bc-c, a ten-line stanza like this: aab-aab-bcb-C. Finally, there was the *virelai*. It resembled the ballade poetically in its tripartite division of a stanza, but deviated musically in that the refrain got started at the outset and returned at the end of each stanza. Thus a three-stanza virelai might look like this: AbbA-bbaA-bbaA.

Note that musically the rondeau and virelai have but two sections, the ballade three. Machaut retained these distinctions, while standardizing the lengths of the stanzas for each form. In each of the three fixed forms, the texts were much shorter than lais or other narratives, and the music, instead of developing continuously as with Machaut's lais, falls into two or three sections which are then repeated in assorted patterns throughout the chanson. Conceptually, then, the fixed forms were uncomplicated. Machaut extended this basic simplicity to the very nature of his melodies, which tended to be more tuneful, folklike, and catchy than those of the lais—qualities heightened by the built-in repetition scheme.

While the bulk of Machaut's virelais are monphonic, all but one of the ballades and rondeaux are polyphonic. In these polyphonic chansons Machaut established a model for accompanied song that influenced composers well into the Renaissance. First the chosen text was provided with a melody. To this were added anywhere from one to three textless parts, which could either be vocalized by other singers or performed instrumentally. Adam de la Halle had done something similar a century before. But where Adam's added parts conformed to the rhythm of the main melody (and so could be sung to the same text in conductus fashion), Machaut distinguished his accompaniments from the tune in virtually every respect. They were designed to complement rather than mirror that tune, and did so both rhythmically and harmonically. Unlike the individual lines of motets, these accompaniments were not designed as self-sufficient entities with their own distinctive rhythmic patterns, but rather as enhancements of the tune.

Italy—A Country With Its Own Ideas

Up to this point the history of polyphony has revolved around France, especially Paris, largely because there was no tradition of notated polyphony in Italy before the 14th century. Within the Italian Church, polyphony was apparently an improvised art. The Italians realized that polyphony could enhance special liturgical occasions, but saw no reason to attempt anything more complicated than note-against-note counterpoint to a chant. Since improvisational techniques were totally adequate for this purpose, there was no need to write down the results. Neither the organum or discantus styles of St. Martial nor the more elaborate organa, clausulae, and motets of the Notre Dame school played a part in Italian liturgical polyphony. Even well into the 14th century, Latin motets or settings of the Mass Ordinary held little interest for Italian composers. Though the reasons are not completely evident, they are surely based on the primary function of the Italian composer: to provide music for social occasions of every sort. The high value placed on the social aspect of music in 14th-century Italy is reflected in the literature from the period, Boccaccio's *Decameron* (1348–53) in particular, which illustrates how much attention the upper classes paid to the improvisation of both poetry and monophonic music.

Italian Forms

Not until c. 1330 does any quantity of polyphonic music appear in Italy. Polyphony's rapid growth paralleled a flourishing of serious poetry in 14th-century Italy: Dante (1265–1321), Petrarch (1304–74), and Boccaccio (1313–75) were the greatest figures. Yet composers of secular polyphony puzzlingly almost entirely neglected the more sophisticated poetic genres *(canzoni* and *sonnetti),* concentrating instead on three relatively simple forms: the *madrigal, caccia,* and *ballata.* The madrigal was an indigenous form bearing no resemblance to the 16th-century madrigal. It contains two distinct sections: in the first, two or three stanzas are presented, all to the same music; in the second, termed the *ritornello,* new music and text appear, the music invariably in a contrasting meter. Thus the overall form is aab or aaab. Madrigal texts are usually "idyllic, pastoral, amatory, or satirical" (as Donald Grout puts it); each of the two or three parts shared the same text, though the upper parts tended to be more elaborate and melismatic.

The ballata replaced the madrigal as the foremost Italian polyphonic secular form in the second half of the 14th century.

During the first half of the century monophonic ballate had served as the chief means of musical expression composed by and for the upper class (again, the *Decameron* offers vivid proof). Like the French fixed forms, the ballata probably originated as a monophonic dance song (the noblemen and ladies of Boccaccio's *Decameron* cultivated music not as high art, but as a social grace). Ballate were in fact formally identical to the French virelai, though this needn't imply a genealogical relationship.

The third major Trecento form was the caccia. It too had a French counterpart, the *chace,* and both were based on canonic technique. But while the chace remained strictly imitative throughout, however many voice parts, the caccia typically had two canonic upper parts supported by a free tenor which normally played no role in the canonic structure. Texts of both chace and cacce were lighter than those of the other forms, often humorous, even licentious; they frequently revolved around a hunt (*caccia*'s literal meaning) of some sort, whether for animals or women. Often imitative elements—shouts and screams, dialogue, bird songs, hunting calls—figured prominently. Through such techniques as hocket and echo effects a clever composer could turn what on paper looks perfectly respectable into aural equivalents that prove unexpectedly obscene. Such mimicry characterized French virelais as well, and also made its way into Italian madrigals and ballate.

Italian Composers

Allied with the two most powerful ruling families of northern Italy in the 14th century, the Visconti in Milan and the Scaligeri in Verona and Padua, were such composers as Magister Piero, Giovanni da Firenze (also known as Giovanni da Cascia), and Jacopo da Bologna, believed to be the teacher of Francesco Landini (c. 1325–1397). Landini's work, like that of his younger contemporaries Nicolo da Perugia, Bartolino da Padova, Andrea da Firenze, and Paolo Tenorista, focused around Florence, the center of Italian music in the second half of the century.

Landini was the most celebrated of all Trecento composers and remains the best-known today. Because Landini's music was so cherished, it comes down in great quantity: the 154 preserved compositions represent about a quarter of the entire surviving repertoire of the Trecento! Whereas the first generation of Trecento composers concentrated exclusively on the madrigal and caccia, all but 13 of Landini's pieces are polyphonic ballate. Tales of his abilities as both composer and virtuoso on many instruments, especially the organetto (small portable organ), reached legendary proportions. Nowhere is Landini more revered than in Giovanni da Prato's *Paradiso degli Alberti* (1389), where he appears as one of the principal characters. Though this work dates from no earlier than 1425, Prato claims to record actual incidents from the year 1389. Of Landini the composer Prato wrote glowingly: "No one had ever heard such beautiful harmonies, and their hearts almost burst from their bosoms." As a performer, his powers were greater still:

"As a thousand birds were singing among the verdant branches, someone asked Francesco to play the organ a little, to see whether the sound would make the birds increase or diminish their song. He did so at once, and a greater wonder followed: for when the sound began many of the birds were seen to fall silent, and gather around as if in amazement, listening for a long time; and then they resumed their song and redoubled it, showing inconceivable delight, and especially one nightingale, who came and perched above the organ on a branch over Francesco's head.''

Landini merits still another claim to fame: blinded since childhood by smallpox, he became the first in a long and distinguished line of sightless organists.

Some Generalizations

In whatever form, Trecento music has a character all its own. Italians seemed unconcerned with mathematical order and rhythmic superstructures, much more preoccupied with sweetness of melody and beauty of sound. French composers conceived their pieces in layers, with each part clearly differentiated from the others, and one part frequently dominant. Quintessential French textures are those of the motet and accompanied song. The Italians, on the other hand, wrote music in which the parts were relatively equal—the vocal duet (sometimes accompanied by a textless contratenor) is a quintessential Italian texture. French/ Italian differences extended to the very nature of melody. A typical French chanson melody appears carefully planned. It is subtle, often jerky in rhythm and relatively undemanding on the singer's technique; the accompanimental parts are designed for textural variety, with little regard for the sometimes acrimonious dissonances and austere progressions that resulted. A typical Italian melody appears spontaneous, far smoother and virtuosic than its French counterpart; the accompanimental parts are designed to provide harmonic richness, to contribute sweetness and suavity to the whole. In short, medieval French music stressed the intellectual, Italian the emotional.

Mannerism

Toward the end of the 14th century, the distinctions between Italian and French music began to narrow, and in favor of the French. Despite the reestablishment of the Papacy in Rome in 1377, the rival Avignon papal court continued to be the major center for production of sacred polyphony; at the same time it became even more important as a center for French secular music. Closely connected to Avignon were the courts of Peter IV (reigned 1336–87) and John I (1387–96), Kings of Aragon, and of Gaston Phebus, Count of Bearn and Foix (1343–91). With their dazzling chivalric society, these courts attracted from all over Europe composers who developed a style of extremes, a style which influenced musicians far beyond the immediate sphere of the Pyrenees. The principal sources of their music are the Chantilly manuscript, copied in the early 15th century in Florence, and manuscripts from Modena and Venice (the Reina Codex). By far the most common form—even among the Italians—is the French ballade, and the dominant language is also French.

Composers vied with one another in stretching notational resources to the breaking point. Since the French notational system allowed for greater rhythmic manipulations, it was used more often in both French and Italian music, though the Italians often retained their own unusual note shapes to obtain still more rhythmic intricacy. Complicated syncopations were introduced, both within and between parts. Meters changed constantly. To assist this latter endeavor, coloration was developed—red, black, and white notes signified different proportions, with some colorful scores as an incidental byproduct. One composer, Baude Cordier, even attempted a visual reflection of his texts. Thus he wrote the ballade "Belle, bonne, sage" in the shape of a heart, while the perpetual canon "Tour par compas suy compose" is in the shape of a circle. Musicians went beyond the rhythmic level to experiment with range, dissonance, and chromaticism. Only in the 20th century has there been a comparable cultivation of music for the virtuoso initiate.

Often these complexities were artificial, existing more on paper than reality (many of the rhythms could have just as easily been notated by simpler means). But while the preoccupation with technique for technique's sake marks a certain decadence, much of this music is also fascinating and satisfying. Donald Grout has aptly described such pieces as "works of refined beauty, with sensitive melodies and delicately colored harmonies, examples of aristocratic art in the best sense of the word."

Spain

Not all polyphonic music of the Ars Nova era originated in France or Italy; yet the influence of these countries, France in particular, was so strong that it shaped musical style throughout the Western world. The Chapel Royal at Barcelona, for instance, was almost entirely dependent upon the papal chapel at Avignon for both its performers and repertoire during the last half of the 14th century: The close relationship between King John I of Catalonia and Aragon (1350–96) and the court at Avignon is but one example.

Spain was not only an enormously active site for courtly musicians throughout the Middle Ages, but also a major center of liturgical polyphony. As noted in the previous chapter, Compostela was the focal point for the Codex Calixtinus, one of the major compilations of early polyphony (c. 1150). During the next two centuries the religious polyphonic action shifted to Toledo, Ripoll, and Tortosa, but the most important manuscript comes from the Cistercian nunnery of Las Huelgas. This collection was copied largely during the first quarter of the 14th century. Among its 186 items are 136 polyphonic works, representing most of the principal genres of the day: organa, motets, conducti (including the only known bitextual conductus), *Benedicamus* settings, and sequences.

As is the case with medieval music in general, very little truly popular Spanish music survives. The earliest collection of Spanish folk songs, *De Musici Libri Septem* (The Seven Books of Music), dates from 1577. But some of the pieces in this great compilation by the blind organist Francisco de Salinas were already quite old. One of them, *Polorum regina,* appears in the c. 1400 *Llibre Vermell* (Red Book), so-called because of the luxurious red velvet binding provided for the manuscript in the 19th century. This manuscript contains 10 short pieces, pilgrim songs and dances, from the famous monastery of Montserrat, the legendary site of the Holy Grail. After night-long vigils at the shrine of Our Lady pilgrims refreshed themselves by performing music written or arranged expressly for this purpose by the monks. As Gilbert Chase relates in his *The Music of Spain,* "All the evidence points to the conclusion that these pilgrim songs were originally folk tunes to which sacred words were added by the monks of Monteserrat."

All but one of the 10 pieces in the collection are dedicated to the Virgin Mary. That exception is the monophonic song *Ad mortem festinamus* (We hasten towards death), the oldest extant musical version of the Dance of Death. There are five other songs (some monophonic, some polyphonic, some in ballade or virelai form) intended for group dancing, perhaps even within the temple itself. Just as interesting are the three *caças,* the earliest Spanish canons, analogous to the French chace and the Italian caccia.

Germany

Germany, habitually conservative, lagged considerably behind other European countries in the development of part music. Far and away the chief medieval figure was the South Tyrolean knight Oswald von Wolkenstein (c. 1377–1445), already mentioned in Chapter 2. In some respects his life paralleled that of Machaut, who died about the time of Wolkenstein's birth. Like Machaut, Wolkenstein worked for kings and was exceptionally well travelled, with sojourns as far afield as Byzantium, Persia, Africa, and Russia; and, like Machaut, Wolkenstein was an important poet as well as a musician, the last representative of the monophonic tradition of the minnesingers (of his 125 compositions, only about a quarter are polyphonic). Also like Machaut, Wolkenstein set the model for an indigenous polyphonic song. Wolkenstein was a great synthesist. He took French and Italian forms and idioms, adding to them a characteristic German love for instruments (many of his pieces included instrumental ritornellos) and folklike flavor. Above all, his music had personality, the personality of a warm, deeply human individual.

Johannes Ciconia

Johannes Ciconia (c. 1335–1411) was in many respects a paradox. Born in Belgium, trained in the French tradition, he nonetheless chose to live in Italy and compose his secular pieces primarily in Italian forms. Living in a secular era, he nonetheless chose to devote the better part of his output to sacred works, including nine Mass movements and 11 motets. Surrounded on all sides by mannerists, Ciconia forged a fresh, more direct style that drew on the strengths of both French and Italian music, allying the French concern for structural unity with Italian mellifluousness and lyric grace. There were new features, too: a rhythmic and melodic terseness, a bass line as much harmonic as melodic in function. Of course, these features were not entirely original; among Ciconia's contemporaries Matteo da Perugia (fl. c. 1400–1418) in particular emerges as a leader in the early 15th-century reaction away from mannerism.

Ciconia stands out as one of the most distinguished and distinctive composers of his time, one whose music deserves much greater recognition. And in at least two respects he appears genuinely innovative. He was the first known composer to regularly write Mass movements in musically related Gloria-Credo pairs. Moreover, he may well have introduced the concept of solo versus choral polyphony, sometimes termed responsorial polyphony. Previous liturgical responsories alternated choral monophony with solo polyphony. Ciconia carried this practice a step further in three of his Mass movements by alternating unaccompanied duets for soloists with three- and four-part motet-like passages (also for soloists), a procedure quickly adopted by his younger contemporaries. Such distinctions were indicated in the scores (though not by Ciconia himself, but by a later scribal hand) by the words *unus*, *duo*, and *chorus*.

But it would be dangerous to hail this as the beginning of a new age, one of choral polyphony. The medieval and Renaissance concept of chorus was nothing like that of today. Eight to 12 singers for polyphony were the normal body employed by most churches throughout the Renaissance, not all of whom necessarily sang together. Two or three singers per part was the usual *maximum*. Even when more than one was placed in a part, all these singers rightfully regarded themselves as soloists (and were so remunerated); the true chorus was singing the chants.

England

Britain's close ties to France were remarked upon in the previous chapter; indeed, thanks to the Norman conquest, the language and culture of the English court and aristocracy remained principally French until the end of the 14th century. Yet by the time of the Worcester Fragments (c. 1300), English composers had attained a characteristic idiom all their own, as that collection attests. Salient features of this idiom included regular phrase structures, dancelike rhythms, folklike tunes, and an attempt to integrate the parts through such means as imitation, voice exchange, and canonic techniques. But the most striking aspect of English polyphony was its harmonies. A love for thirds and sixths contributed sweetness and fullness of sound, while a tendency to rely on major tonalities instead of church modes lent the music a modern flavor. By favoring homorhythmic textures and single texts, the British emphasized melody and harmony over rhythm, in defiance of the French predilection (most evident in the motet) for independent lines, harsh dissonances, and polytextuality.

These stylistic trends intensified with the passing years. Plentiful proof is contained in the only other large English collection from the Middle Ages, the Old Hall Manuscript. This preserves a group of works spanning approximately the years 1350–1420, a repertoire dominated by Mass movements. It documents the almost exclusively liturgical nature of surviving English medieval polyphony.

The major exception is the *carol*. Originally the carol, like the fixed forms in France and Italy, was almost certainly a monophonic dance song with refrain, but by the early 1400's, the time of the first surviving carols with music, the carol had stabilized into a strophic polyphonic genre, usually for two or three voice parts. All the stanzas were sung to the same music. These were interspersed with a contrasting refrain called the *burden*, which appeared at the beginning and after every stanza (sometimes there was more than one burden). An alternation between two and three parts, and between soloists and chorus, was typical. Form, not subject matter, earmarks the carol. Usually the text was religious (though non-liturgical), but could encompass any conceivable topic, even amatory ones. An especially famous carol is the stirring *Deo gratias Anglia,* written to celebrate the English victory at Agincourt in 1415. While carols were rarely if ever based upon actual folk material, they nonetheless give the impression of art music in a popular style.

To a far greater extent than their Continental counterparts, English composers c. 1400 were clearly at the threshold of a new era. Some of the Old Hall pieces, especially those by Power and Dunstable, can in fact more accurately be classified as Renaissance than medieval. It is with them that a discussion of the musical Renaissance properly begins.

Performance Considerations

The problems involved in the performance of late medieval polyphony are not so different than those of earlier part-music (see Chapter 4). In at least one crucial respect, matters are far simpler: rhythms in the Ars Nova period and beyond are rarely ambiguous. All told, the chief difficulties boil down to two basic considerations: the disposition of voices and instruments.

Manuscripts are of little help here since they never specify instruments or vocal types. That leaves only one clue to determine if music is vocal or instrumental—the presence of a text. And even this is unreliable. In Notre Dame organa, for instance, only the tenor is texted. Does that automatically prescribe instrumental realization of the upper parts? Clearly not, for there were no instruments admissible to medieval churches that could manage the parts, and besides, vocal participation is implied by the very character of the lines and derivation of the music (see Chapter 4). Even contemporary theorists attest that these upper parts were sung. Probably they were vocalized on the corresponding vowel in the tenor part; certainly the effect produced by changing vowel sounds is most impressive.

There is every reason to suppose that performances of the secular art song repertoire were flexible, dictated by the resources at hand. Sometimes a part exists in a textless version in one manuscript, yet is furnished with a text in another. A textless part might be either vocally *or* instrumentally realized, just as a texted part could be doubled or even replaced by instruments. There is also the possibility of instrumental heterophony. Vocal pieces were now and then entirely played by instruments, often with embellishments added to the main melodic lines. Some music was even designed so that an accompanimental part could be eliminated or substituted for without in any way damaging the integrity of the piece. A final possibility was alternation of instruments and/or voices. (If David Munrow is to be believed, female vocal participation at the professional level—either in church or court—was rare before 1450.)

But flexibility needn't imply license. Almost all medieval polyphony was soloist's music, and there is no need for more than one or two voices or instruments per part. If instruments are used, they should be chosen according to range from the ranks of the *bas* (soft) instruments; loud instruments such as brasses and double reeds had no place in a sophisticated art.

The most far-reaching accomplishment of Western medieval music was the move from an oral to a notated tradition. Only by such a step could the elaborate polyphony which distinguishes Western music from that of all other cultures have evolved. This new polyphonic music demanded a special class of musician, one not only technically proficient but able to read his or her own parts. Thus there evolved two distinct classes of singers and instrumentalists: those that were musically literate, and those that were not. The first class was made up of practitioners of high art music, the second class of popular entertainers. These distinctions endure today. Many pop, rock, and (at least until recently) jazz musicians cannot read music; they have no compelling reason to learn.But for classical musicians literacy is essential. The impact of notation upon Western music history cannot be overestimated.

SELECTED RECORDINGS

General Anthology

DOUCE DAME: MUSIC OF COURTLY LOVE FROM MEDIEVAL FRANCE AND ITALY
The Waverly Consort; Michael Jaffee, director
Vanguard VSD 71179
Includes anonymous instrumental pieces and secular songs by Machaut, Jacopo da Bologna, Landini, Lorenzo da Firenze

---

The Waverly Consort's *Douce Dame* is the most stimulating and satisfying of the single-disc surveys. Like their *Cantigas* album (discussed in Chapter 2), they display marvelous theatricality, a broad range of performance styles (including choral realizations), and a welcome lightness of touch. Occasionally the group goes a bit overboard (they even appropriate Arabic instruments and heterophony to two Machaut virelais—not even Binkley goes this far), but their skill and enthusiasm invariably save the day.

ROMAN DE FAUVEL
Studio der Frühen Musik; Thomas Binkley, director; Jean Bollery, speaker
EMI Reflexe 1C 063-30103
Clemencic Consort; René Clemencic, director; René Zosso, reciter
Harmonia Mundi HM 994

The two *Fauvel* albums provide ample opportunity for interesting comparisons. Both present a generous selection of verses and music, but while Binkley's reciter *speaks* all the poetry, Clemencic's counterpart sometimes speaks, and sometimes sings to a drone in a manner suggestive of *sprechgesang*. Each performance is adventurous and highly entertaining. As might be expected, Binkley opts for heterophony and improvisation in a number of places; yet even at his most daring, he rarely oversteps the boundaries of good taste. Not Clemencic. He seems intent on featuring every member of his vast instrumentarium—either singly or in ensemble. Ostensibly Binkley and Clemencic both view *Fauvel* as a sort of protest play with music. But Clemencic carries satire to burlesque.

Machaut
MASS; SECULAR WORKS
The Purcell Choir with instrumental ensemble; directed by Grayston Burgess
L'Oiseau-Lyre SOL 310
CHANSONS I/II
Studio der Frühen Musik; Thomas Binkley, director
Volume I (monophonic), EMI Reflexe 1C 063-30106; Volume II (polyphonic), EMI Reflexe 1C 063-30109
MACHAUT AND HIS CONTEMPORARIES
Early Music Consort of London directed by David Munrow
EMI ASD 3454 (Volume I of The Art of Courtly Love)
Secular songs by Machaut, Jehan de Lescurel, Pierre des Molins, and F. Andrieu

---

Thankfully, there are a healthy number of satisfying Machaut recordings. The interest generated of late by this man may be gleaned from the sheer size of his discographic catalogue—far greater than that of any other medieval composer.

An ideal starting point for the Machaut collector is the 1969 Burgess L'Oiseau-Lyre disc. This contains the most often recorded large-scale medieval piece, Machaut's Mass, in its only satisfactory recording known to me. The performance is entirely unaccompanied, the performers all men. Instead of repeating each section of the *Kyrie*, as was customary, organ elaborations from the late 14th-century Faenza Codex are substituted. The singing is extremely persuasive: slightly nasal in sound, with crisp rhythms and impressive forward thrust united with a gratifying lyric flow. L'Oiseau-Lyre has gone to pains on every level, even to the hiring of Dr. Daffyd Evans as pronunciation supervisor and the noted scholar Frank Lloyd Harrison as artistic director and music editor. On Side 2 a lovely selection of Machaut's secular works, although elegantly sung, is too often burdened with heavy-handed instrumental support.

Thomas Binkley and his group contribute two characteristically stimulating Machaut albums, one of polyphonic music, the other primarily monophonic. No Arabicisms intrude here, but there are the familiar improvised instrumental accompaniments on the monophonic disc, and both discs succumb to a surfeit of the group's annoying mannerisms: white vocal tone, quirky articulation (superfluous slurs, slides, staccati), and both overrefinement and virtuosity for virtuosity's sake. Excessively ''big,'' close-up recorded sound does not help matters. Nonetheless, there is much to admire. Particularly rewarding is the performance of the complete *Lay de la fonteinne* on the first disc. The odd-numbered monophonic stanzas are rendered convincingly by Andrea Ramm to lute accompaniment, while the three-part canons of the even-numbered stanzas are sometimes sung one to a part (usually by girl soloists), sometimes by girls' chorus.

From the strictly interpretive point of view, probably the most successful available recordings devoted to Machaut and his French contemporaries are those found in the Munrow anthologies: a collection of motets, including two by Vitry and four by Machaut, on the Ars Nova portion of the Gothic Era album; and a selection of songs, most by Machaut, as Volume I of the Courtly Love set. The musicality or technical accomplishment of these performances cannot be sufficiently praised. Nearly every conceivable human mood gets projected with a sure hand; rarely does one feel that the conceptions are anything but felicitous.Only the occasional inappropriate use of loud *(haut)* instruments blemishes the perfection.

Italy

LANDINI: SELECTED WORKS
Studio der Frühen Musik; Thomas Binkley, director
EMI Reflexe 1C 063-30113
ECCO LA PRIMAVERA: FLORENTINE MUSIC OF THE 14TH
CENTURY
Early Music Consort of London directed by David Munrow
Argo ZRG 642
Includes songs by Landini (7), Magister Piero, Giovanni da Firenze,
Lorenzo da Firenze, and Jacopo da Bologna
MUSIC FROM THE TIME OF BOCCACCIO'S "DECAMERON"
Musica Reservata of London, conducted by John Beckett
Philips 802 904
Includes songs by Landini (6), Giovanni da Firenze, and Gherardello
da Firenze, plus seven instrumental selections
DECAMERON: BALLATE MONODIQUES DE L'ARS NOVA
FLORENTINE
Esther Lamandier, voice, portative organ, harp, fiddle, and lute
Astrée AS 56
Monophonic ballate by Landini, Gherardello da Firenze, Lorenzo da
Firenze, and Anon

All four listed recordings of mainstream Italian repertoire are highly recommendable, both for the music and the performances. Since those by the Studio der Frühen Musik, Early Music Consort, and Musica Reservata for the most part represent the individual styles of these groups at their considerable best (though I could do without the annoying machine-gun enunciation of von Ramm in rapid numbers), and since those styles have been dealt with at length elsewhere in this book, further commentary seems superfluous here. Taken as a group, they afford an absorbing compendium of performance possibilities.

These three albums deserve supplementation by Lamandier's disc, which is devoted solely to the important Trecento tradition of monophonic ballate. As in her *Cantigas* record (see Chaper 2), Lamandier does everything herself: she sings, and she plays the four most common accompaniment instruments, all superbly well. Her vocal mastery is especially astonishing. Yet this recording, for all its excellence, is not as satisfying as the later *Cantigas* album. Part of the problem is the voice itself, which is whiter, more boyish in tone, less personal in timbre (more akin to von Ramm) than in the *Cantigas* recording. Additional difficulties accrue from the emphasis on virtuosity: some extremely brisk tempos result in unintelligible words and too many di-di-di-di, da-da-da-da vocalizations. And there is a rhythmic laxness, understandable for the vague neumatic notation of the troubadour/trouvère repertoire, but less justifiable in the precisely measured rhythms of this Italian music. Obviously Lamandier views these pieces from the context of the oral performance tradition, where rhythmic flexibility is expected.

Late Medieval—Manneristic and Transitional

LATE FOURTEENTH CENTURY AVANT GARDE
Early Music Consort of London directed by David Munrow
EMI ASD 3621

MATTEO DA PERUGIA: SECULAR MUSIC
The Medieval Ensemble of London directed by Peter and Timothy Davies
L'Oiseau-Lyre Florilegium DSLO 577

JOHANNES CICONIA: FRENCH, ITALIAN, AND LATIN WORKS (SACRED AND SECULAR)
Studio der Frühen Musik; Thomas Binkley, director
EMI Reflexe 1C 063-3012

In the mannerist repertoire, as in so much before, Munrow and his Early Music Consort garner pride of place. Indeed, their Avant Garde album provides one of the most spectacular demonstrations of their achievements. One would scarcely know how incredibly difficult this music is, so entirely natural are the performances. No longer must the listener writhe in agony while the musicians struggle to realize the manifold complexities; now the music can be appreciated on its own substantial merit. For starters, sample Solage's rondeau *Fumeux fume* (Fumy fumes), with its startling low tessitura and eccentric chromatic harmonies. Baritone Geoffrey Shaw, accompanied by Oliver Brookes on bass rebec and Munrow himself on bass kortholt, capture its smoky flavor perfectly. Michael Freeman supervised the pronunciation for the entire Courtly Love project.

Not too many other worthwhile recordings of this mannered music exist; the selections on the French side of the Musica Reservata's *Hundred Years' War* album, for instance, though at times brilliant musically, seem far too acrid in approach.

Don't miss the Studio der Frühen Musik's Ciconia disc. This is one of their very finest efforts, with minimal affectation and maximal sensitivity. Von Ramm displays remarkable bravura; I know of no better introduction to her artistry. And Ciconia emerges as a major figure, master of every style. His secular music is strikingly personal; mercurial and virtuosic, yet wonderfully melodious, with a refined and expressive harmonic language. *O rosa bella* attains an almost Monteverdian scope and power. A richly sonorous quality imbues the Latin works, with a splendidly effective contrast between homophonic and imitative textures.

Spain

MISSA DE SANCTA MARIA
The Ambrosian Singers; Denis Stevens, conductor
Dover HCR 5263

LLIBRE VERMELL
Included in two collections: (1) *Music in Catalonia.* Capilla Musical y Escolania de Santa Cruz del Valle de los Caidos; Atrium Musicae; directed by Jose Luis Ochoa de Olza
Musical Heritage Society Orpheus OR 433; also available as Harmonia Mundi HM 10051
(2) *Secular Music c. 1300.* Early Music Quartet; Thomas Binkley, director
Telefunken SAWT 9504

Recordings of Spanish repertoire offer slim pickings. Best of the liturgical albums is Stevens's long-out-of-print Dover disc, well worth a search. Stevens has assembled seven items from the Las Huelgas Codex, encompassing both chant and polyphony. The polyphonic music embraces a wider stylistic range; much of it sounds surprisingly modern considering the probable date of 1300 or before. Stevens directs a quartet of first-rate soloists (some familiar from the Pro Cantione Antiqua) in an impressive performance, modestly supported by organ. The Early Music Quartet's rendition of the *Llibre* makes use of a boys' chorus. Bright and inventive, brimming with insights (for example, the mocking nature of the Dance of Death), but with few extravagances, this forms a most agreeable conclusion to the group's enchanting Secular Music c. 1300 album (see also Chapter 2).

Germany

WOLKENSTEIN: LIEDER
Soloists, instrumentalists, Chamber Choir Walter von der Vogelweide; Othmar Costa, conductor
Telefunken Das Alte Werk 6.41139
WOLKENSTEIN: LIEDER
Studio der Frühen Musik; Thomas Binkley, director
EMI Reflexe 1C 063-30101

The two Wolkenstein collections have often been praised in relation to the composer's monophonic output; but in addition, their polyphonic contents, comprising the better part of each album, are just as winning. The music is in some respects made to order for Binkley and comrades, and they make the most of every opportunity for technical display and graphic delineation of the texts. Especially telling in these respects is von Ramm's quicksilver *Der mai,* with embellishments in the recorder and fiddle playing mirroring the singer. Doris Linser's version under Costa's direction is slower and more flowing, playing down both the humor and virtuosity of the music, though sung with great beauty. In general, Costa's renditions tend to be earthier and more strongly rhythmic than Binkley's. Both discs are irresistible.

England

MISSA SALVE SANCTA PARENS
Ambrosian Singers; Denis Stevens, conductor
Dover HCR 5263
With the Spanish *Missa de Sancta Maria*
THE WORCESTER FRAGMENTS
Accademia Monteverdiana; Denis Stevens, director
Nonesuch H-71308
MUSIC IN HONOR OF ST. THOMAS OF CANTERBURY: MEDIEVAL CAROLS, CONDUCTUS, MOTETS, MASSES, AND PLAINSONG
Academia Monteverdiana; Trinity Boys' Choir; Denis Stevens, director
Nonesuch H-71292
MEDIEVAL ENGLISH CAROLS AND ITALIAN DANCES
New York Pro Musica; Noah Greenberg, director
American Decca 79148

MEDIEVAL ENGLISH LYRICS
Assorted soloists and instrumentalists
Argo ZRG 5443
Pieces span late-12th century to mid-15th century
NOW WE MAKE MERTHE: MEDIEVAL CAROLS
The Purcell Consort of Voices; Boys of All Saints, Margaret Street;
instrumentalists; Grayston Burgess, director
Argo ZRG 526
Christmas songs from 12th century to mid-16th century; includes
music from England, Spain, France, and Germany

Equally irresistible are the two Denis Stevens Nonesuch anthologies already discussed in Chapter 4. The late medieval selections
are every bit as good as the earlier ones, and together these
albums provide an excellent sampling of the stylistic range of
English medieval music. The last item on the Worcester album is
a moving four-part setting of the Introit *Salve sancta parens*.
Stevens takes this piece and links it with five late-13th-century
Mass movements from the Worcester Fragments to form an
exceptionally handsome Sarum Lady-Mass on his Dover album.
The all-male singing is as exquisite as the music, and entirely
unaccompanied save for the Sequentia. Well worth a search.

If your budget allows for only a single album of carols, that
choice should be made from one of the Argo discs. Like the EMI
Courtly Love collection and the L'Oiseau-Lyre Machaut record,
these manifest painstaking care on every level. Frank Lloyd
Harrison served as music editor and advisor, while Eric J.
Dobson adopted a similar role with the poetry. Moreover, the
texts are sung in pronunciation as close to authentic Middle
English as modern scholarship allows. Hearing familiar pieces
sung in medieval pronunciation of your native language produces
a startling and at first unsettling effect. But after a few moments
the advantages emerge and a smile of delight creeps over the
face, a smile which grows larger as the sheerly *musical* quality of
these performances becomes evident. They are beyond re-
proach, and the reluctance to use instruments except when truly
necessary (especially in the all-English *Medieval English Lyrics*)
enhances the final product. Lest this sound suspicious to instrument fanatics, one need only compare the unaccompanied Argo
version of the Agincourt Carol (on *Medieval English Lyrics*) with
those by the New York Pro Musica and Musica Reservata
(Hundred Years' War). These latter groups go with all the forces
they've got, including percussion, with stirring consequences.
The Argo forces stick to six solo voices, and—amazingly—
generate as much power and additional eloquence. Vivid indeed is
the contrast between the full-throated full group on refrains and
the more restrained individual soloists in the verses, the whole
abetted by the piquant medieval pronunciation. The instrumental
myth is dispelled.

6

THE RENAISSANCE: *A Brief Overview*

When applied to music, traditional concepts of a renaissance do not fit. The established picture of the Renaissance derives from Jacob Burckhardt's monumental *The Civilization of the Renaissance in Italy* (1860), a picture almost wholly conditioned by the political and intellectual history of a single country, Italy. While it is true that Italy dominated most arts in the 15th and 16th centuries, the country produced no composer of international stature in this era until well into the 16th century. By this time musical language was moving rapidly toward the new Baroque style. The very word "renaissance" focuses the problem when dealing with music. The word means "rebirth," and indeed writers and artists of the 15th and 16th centuries viewed their time as an age reviving the attainments of ancient Greece and Rome. They made many discoveries of Greek and Roman art and literature which became models for their own works. But there were no comparable discoveries of ancient music and the teachings of Greek musical theory could hardly be reborn, for they had been retained through the Middle Ages. Precisely the same sort of compositions that predominated during the 14th century—masses, motets, settings of secular poetry—continued to do so in the 15th and 16th centuries.

Yet the concept of a musical Renaissance is perfectly valid, and would very likely be wholeheartedly endorsed by those men whose music falls under that designation. For if there was not a literal "rebirth" of ancient music, there was what was perceived as a rebirth of the human spirit, the movement known as *humanism*. The depression of the 14th century gave way to far-reaching optimism. "The world is coming to its senses as if awakening out of a deep sleep," wrote the scholar Erasmus (c. 1466–1536). Each generation saw its own art as superior to anything that came before (a far cry from present-day artistic attitudes). Johannes Tinctoris, chapelmaster to the King of Naples, captured this spirit well in these lines from his counterpoint treatise of 1477: "Although it seems beyond belief, there does not exist a single piece of music, not composed within the last forty years, that is regarded by the learned as worth hearing."

Renaissance vs. Medieval Style

Obviously a new kind of music was being written. Its most characteristic and revolutionary feature was the focus upon melody, rather than upon rhythm. In medieval polyphony—the isorhythmic motet being the classic example—rhythmic patterns were layered upon one another. Melodic lines evidently usually were composed *successively;* certain parts could be replaced or omitted without damaging the underlying structure. Even medieval dissonance was rhythmic in basis. Only consonances were allowed on strong beats, but virtually any degree of dissonance was tolerated in between. Composers of the Renaissance devised a style in which melodic lines took precedence. Insofar as possible, no one part dominated; every part was intrinsic and equal to every other. Good examples are masses, motets, and madrigals where the same text appears in each part but at slightly different times. When medieval musicians superimposed rhythmic structures, they often tried to clearly differentiate each part from the other. Renaissance composers, on the other hand, aimed at parts which were not only equal in importance, but complementary. When one line went up another would go down, forming a constantly intertwining series of peaks and valleys. Such close interaction naturally required careful planning and necessitated a *simultaneous* style of composition in which all the parts were conceived and written at the same time.

The Renaissance emphasis on melody had a number of important consequences. Dissonance was regarded primarily from a melodic standpoint, and was approached or resolved with great care. As a result, Renaissance music tends to have a very high consonance level. Since consonances possess considerably less tension than dissonances, and since acoustical experiments show that humans perceive consonances as farther away than dissonances of the same volume and source, classic Renaissance polyphony strikes us for very good reason as both ethereal and remote. These qualities are intensified by the lack of strong rhythmic accents and the absence of thundering climaxes. Instead, polyphony of the High Renaissance—the so-called International Style—strives for a continuously flowing, gently undulating texture comprised of shapely individual lines. Rhythm was regulated by a steady pulse termed the *tactus;* tempo changes generally related mathematically to that basic tactus. Renaissance composers achieved rich and resonant harmonies. But these harmonies were largely dictated by the intervallic relationships of one line to another, not by the concept of chords in the modern sense. Nor was Renaissance music directed towards a large-scale harmonic goal; tonal planning in the sense of Beethoven and the great symphonists was not part of the Renaissance aesthetic. Thus we cannot expect a forcible sense of development, of tonal inevitability, from this music; Renaissance music tends to be harmonically as well as rhythmically static, and tableaux

thereby achieves its timeless, peaceful quality. This relative lack of drama extends to the treatment of the text itself: not until quite late in the Renaissance was there a concerted attempt to graphically bring out the meaning of individual words, or to do more than suggest the general mood of a given text. Renaissance polyphony was a subtle art.

Toward the middle of the 16th century the International Style began to dissolve. Each of the major musical countries developed it own indigenous styles and genres. Whatever the form, an attempt was made to express images and feelings in the most vivid possible manner. Music for soloists with accompaniment grew increasingly prominent; with it inevitably came the demise of equality of part-writing. Violent contrasts and dissonances, melodic fragmentation, and extremes of harmony signalled the end of one era and the emergence of another—what we now term the Baroque.

Huge quantities of Renaissance music survive, a fact that cannot simply be attributed to better means of preservation. In the Middle Ages the creation, performance, and audience for polyphony was restricted to a very limited circle, mostly confined to the large churches and wealthy courts. In the Renaissance this circle broadened immensely, so that art music became an integral part of the life of all but the lowest social classes, even in the smallest churches and towns. Rare was the town without its own band. Numerous musical academies were established, from which a truly professional class of performers emerged. Whereas in the Middle Ages musical anonymity was the rule, in the Renaissance individuals were recognized and applauded. Fame extended not only to the outstanding composer but also to the virtuoso instrumentalist and singer. In addition, the invention of printing revolutionized music. By the mid-16th century music printing was well established throughout the Western musical world. The rapid appearance of ''how to'' books for mastering a wide variety of instruments and other musical subjects attests to the rapid proliferation of informed amateur musicians. This huge demand for instruments in turn led to the establishment of great houses of instrument builders.

Some Performance Guidelines

By the 15th century, rhythm and pitch, those perennial bugaboos of medieval music, largely ceased to be ambiguous. This is not to say that Renaissance music has no performance problems; far from it. Many musical aspects now taken for granted—tempo, dynamics, phrasing and articulation, expression, instrumentation (even the indication that instruments were or were not to be used)—rarely if ever were designated in the Renaissance. Since music cannot exist without these qualities, their implementation must rely on common sense for what is appropriate for the particular piece and performing situation.

During the last two decades musical scholars have been digging deeply into archives from the Renaissance period. Slowly but inexorably the accumulated knowledge thereby obtained has forced performers to change many of their preconceived notions about the performance of this music—the sacred polyphony in particular. Those two notions that require the most revision relate to constitution of vocal groups and the use of instruments.

Sacred Music

Up until fairly recently the normal modern-day realization of a Renaissance mass or motet enlisted the services of a sizable mixed chorus (50 or 100 vocalists was not unusual), often reinforced by a doggedly colorful instrumental contingent. Yet it becomes more and more clear that Renaissance music was not generally sung (or played) by large groups. The average church or chapel during most of the period employed a chorus of eight to 12 singers; 16 or more was exceptional. Nor were all these singers regularly utilized at the same time. Just as a baseball team might maintain 25 players, but only field nine at a time, so a cathedral might keep 12 singers on the payroll, yet seldom call upon more than six or eight at once. The extra numbers served as insurance in times of illness or other unpredictable absences, and for those special occasions which did require the full ensemble. This means that a standard performance of sacred polyphony enlisted only one to three singers per part. Whether or not an individual part was sung by more than one person, all these singers of polyphony were considered "soloists."

Through most of the Renaissance, churches had barely more use for instruments in combination with voices than they did in the Middle Ages. By the mid-15th century organs had achieved a technical standard permitting them to play with or alternate with a group of singers. But this does not indicate they were regularly so used. Many important churches, including those at Cambrai and the Sistine Chapel, did not even posses organs. Those that did (especially the Spanish churches) may have reserved their organs for processional functions and for preludes and interludes such as *offertories*. Often the organ was situated in such a fashion that the organist could not see the choir. Indeed, though we know that many courts and cathedrals employed fairly large staffs of instrumentalists, these musicians, at least through the greater part of the Renaissance, performed mainly at processionals (often not even inside the church itself) and at special festive occasions. There are no compelling reasons to think that instruments (with the possible exception of the organ) served a substantive function in sacred polyphonic music such as masses and motets until the very end of the Renaissance, and even then only in certain locales and situations. The instrumentalists had their role, but this was not primarily to accompany sacred polyphony.

As had long been the tradition, singing in churches was a male province—nunneries were the only acceptable exception. The high parts could be taken either by boys or male sopranos (and in the late 16th century by castrati). In England and the Franco-Flemish countries boy sopranos were a cherished tradition; many of the greatest composers began their careers (as did Haydn and Schubert) as choirboys.

Secular Music

Secular music was another story. Female musicians, who until well into the 16th century were probably largely relegated to courtesan status in European courts, toward the beginning of the 16th century began to achieve considerable fame for their purely musical abilities. For instance, Isabella d'Este, the Marchioness of Mantua (1474–1539), was not merely an enthusiastic patroness of the arts and instrument collector, but also an accomplished singer, lutenist, and keyboard player. Pope Paul III maintained several women among his private musicians. Probably the most famous women of all were the *concerto delle dame* of Duke Alfonso II d'Este of Ferrara, one of whom, Laura Pevarara, was the dedicatee of a sizable quantity of madrigals.

Claudio Monteverdi (1567–1643), a leader of the transition from the late Renaissance to the early Baroque, and one of the greatest madrigalists in both eras.

More important than any names was the conception of music which demanded a female voice. Before the mid-16th century nearly all high parts, whether or not they were actually sung by women, could be managed comfortably by male falsettos. But the Ferrarese composer Nicola Vicentino (1511–72) wrote madrigals which ascended beyond the limits of the male voice range. Claudio Monteverdi, too, exploits the new-found potential of the female voice in his first book of madrigals (1587). This vogue for the sound of women sopranos manifested itself in a curious way within the church. Women, of course, were prohibited from participation in church music, and boy sopranos were not a viable substitution. The only acceptable approximation was provided by castrati; so beloved was their timbre that any moral objections to castration were conveniently overlooked. Castrati became so popular that they were soon put to use by composers of the new art of opera, who managed to devise music uniquely suited to their peculiar qualities. (For more information see Owen Jander's article "Singing" in *The New Grove*.)

Instruments and instrumental music came into prominence as never before. Stylized dance music became popular, as did music for ensembles and individual instruments. Instruments also had prominent roles in secular song, though in pieces such as madrigals there was no essential need for them. Once again circumstances—the type of music, the occasion, available resources, the social strata of the performers and the audience—dictated the exact nature of the realization. The same considerations set forth for the performance of secular music of the 14th century (see Chapter 5) for the most part apply with equal validity to the 15th and 16th centuries.

Modern-day re-creations of Renaissance polyphony could radically be improved if two simple considerations were observed: fewer singers and fewer instruments. The sound ideal was an *a cappella* (unaccompanied) ensemble of equal parts. If all the parts are to emerge clearly in complex polyphony, then there should not be too many singers on any one part. The vocal quality must be free of pervasive vibrato, which serves only to muddy the texture. If instruments are used to double voice lines, they must do so discreetly, without bringing attention to any one line; mixed orchestration, such as krummhorns on one line, recorders on another, emphasizes the individuality, not the equality, of a given part, and therefore should be avoided.

The written score was never intended to be reproduced slavishly. Even the actual pitch could be altered. There were two basic ways: the first was *musica ficta,* the specialized application of unwritten accidentals (e.g. sharps and flats) to existing notes. The second was embellishment, which at times could become highly elaborate. Both were expected from performers of all types of music. Much more research needs to be done on these practices—at present, we simply do not know enough to do more than guess in many situations. But informed guesses are better than nothing, and it would be stimulating to have more liberal treatments of ficta and embellishment available on record for our appraisal. These considerations hardly exhaust the list of difficulties presented to 20th-century editors and performers of Renaissance music. Such a basic consideration as the proper underlay of text to music can often be extremely vexing.

The Renaissance in Perspective

There are today probably enough recordings of Renaissance music to occupy a listener full time for several years. But it would be presumptuous to think that this largesse provides more than an inkling of the full accomplishment of Renaissance composers. Consider: of Palestrina's 105 masses only eight are listed in the most recent Schwann catalog; of Obrecht's approximately 25 just three; of Lasso's more than 50 but one. Some very fine composers—Brumel, Clemens, and Compère to name a few—do not even have an entire disc devoted to their music. The situation scarcely improves when we consider the availability on record of Josquin's 100 motets, Palestrina's 250, or Lasso's 500. Imagine the picture of Beethoven we would have if we could only hear three of his piano sonatas, two of his string quartets, or one of his symphonies. How well could we comprehend Mozart's operatic art if but one opera was within easy access? The picture is even fainter than it appears on the surface, for experts estimate that perhaps only ten percent of the music composed during the Renaissance survives.

7

THE EARLY RENAISSANCE

A New Style

For most people the Renaissance has become identified with a single country: Italy. With music, however, the story is somewhat different—an international Renaissance style was first developed by composers from England, Burgundy, France, and Flanders, and it was not until well into the 16th century that Italy produced an important group of Renaissance composers of her own.

Tinctoris, when praising the music of his time as superior to anything yet conceived, singled out the Englishman John Dunstable (c. 1380/90–1453) and the Burgundians Guillaume Dufay (c. 1400–1474) and Gilles Binchois (c. 1400–c. 1460) as the creators and most important early representatives of a new musical style—that which we today label Renaissance. History bears out Tinctoris's judgment.

The English

Of the many composers represented in the Old Hall Manuscript, the major collection of English music from the early 15th century, two stand out: Dunstable (or Dunstaple) and his slightly older contemporary Leonel Power (c. 1370/85–1445). All of Power's surviving compositions are sacred: approximately 50 Mass movements and motets. Dunstable's output is more varied, and in fact encompasses all the principal categories of composition from his time: isorhythmic motets, Mass Ordinary sections, secular songs (only two), and settings of miscellaneous liturgical texts, totalling some 60 works in all. Both Power and Dunstable organized entire Mass Ordinaries around a single chant tune, which appeared in the tenor of each movement. This chant melody either could occur in isorhythmic fashion, or in a free, non-repeating rhythmic pattern. Either way, a very important principle was at work: the same chant melody served to unify all the movements of the Mass. Such masses were termed cyclic, since a given tune pervaded the entire work. Any melody—chant or otherwise—that served as the basis of a polyphonic composition was termed a *cantus firmus*. The use of a cantus firmus was as old as polyphony itself. Renaissance composers revitalized the practice so that cantus firmus technique became the major approach to Mass composition in the 15th century.

English polyphony of that century most impresses for the same reason that earlier English music did: its rich, euphonious quality. This effect was achieved through full triads, extended passages of block chords, and a low dissonance quotient. English composers frequently varied their full textures with duets for two soloists. They also developed their own melodic style. Fourteenth-century French melodies tended to be nervous and jumpy, Italian melodies elegantly decorated yet static. The English wrote supple, graceful, often spontaneous-sounding melodies that always seemed to be going somewhere, yet thoroughly charmed the listener as they moved toward that destination. "An incredible sweetness" marvelled the Burgundian court poet Martin le Franc over Dunstable's music in 1441. Evidently his music had lost none of its appeal by Tinctoris's time, for that composer declared it "fit not only for men and heroes, but even for immortal gods."

The Burgundian School

British composers from the first half of the 15th century, Dunstable foremost among them, are heavily represented in continental sources. Their primary and longest-lasting influence was upon those composers representing the Burgundian school, named after the four Dukes of Burgundy.

These Dukes—Philip the Bold (d. 1404), John the Fearless (d. 1419), Philip the Good (d. 1467), and Charles the Bold (d. 1477)—though ostensibly feudal vassals to the King of France, in actuality wielded nearly as much power as the King himself. They not only ruled Burgundy in east central France, but also territories encompassing most of what are today Holland, Belgium, northeastern France, Luxembourg, and Lorraine. All were avid patrons of both art and music, setting the trend for nobles of the time, notes Donald Grout, by establishing "a *chapel*, with an accessory corps of composers, singers, and instrumentalists who furnished music for church services, probably also contributed to the secular entertainment of the court, and accompanied their master on his journeys." Such chapels were imitated by popes, emperors, and kings, and provided— along with the cathedrals—the principal means of support for the professional musician.

Of those musicians known to have regularly served one of the Dukes of Burgundy, Gilles Binchois is today the best remembered. Most representative are his 55 polyphonic *chansons*, elegant and sophisticated songs which, to again quote Grout, "excel in the expression of a tender melancholy, just touched with sensuous longing."

But clearly the greatest and most cosmopolitan musician of his time was Guilliame Dufay. Like so many fellow composers, Dufay received his basic musical background while a choirboy at a cathedral school, that of Cambrai. He spent his early career as a singer in the Papal Chapel. He also happened to be a man of broad learning, studying canon law in France. Like Machaut, Dufay became an ordained priest, and seems to have supported himself largely as a church official, notably as canon of the cathedral at Cambrai. He composed in all the major genres of the day, sacred and secular, with uniform excellence. Dufay appropriated the forms and styles of previous generations, transforming them into something richer and more malleable. For instance, he took the isorhythmic motet, by then a dying genre, and resuscitated it as an appropriate vehicle for the celebration of important state and church events. From the English Dufay learned the technique of unifying a Mass Ordinary through a single cantus firmus. But Dufay went several steps further. He limited himself neither to a chant or sacred cantus firmus; secular tunes served just as well. He also expanded the normal texture from three parts to four. By adding an additional part below the borrowed tenor Dufay could build a strong bass foundation, freed of the restrictions imposed by a preexistent melody; he could consequently far more readily control his music's harmonic movement on both the small and large scale.

The Mass *Se la face ay pale,* from about 1450, provides a stunning example of Dufay's mastery of large-scale structure. As far as is known, this was the first Mass to be based on a secular tune. That tenor derives from Dufay's own ballade *Se la face ay pale* (Renaissance masses were typically named for the tune or piece on which they were based). In the fashion of the old isorhythmic motet, Dufay's cantus firmus tenor appears in longer note values than the other parts. Sometimes it is given complete; other times just portions are quoted; some sections omit it entirely. At one point in both the *Gloria* and *Credo* it is even accelerated to produce a sense of climax. Dufay, then, uses his secular tenor to order the form of his Mass. He adopts one further unifying technique, again taken from his English predecessors: the head motif, a brief motive placed at the beginning of each movement.

It might seem bold, but hardly far-fetched for Howard Brown to claim "Dufay formed the central musical language of the Renaissance . . .He led the way in giving to Franco-Netherlandish music a new sonority based on full triads, harmonic direction, and a careful control of dissonance; a new kind of melody composed in freely flowing rhythms and gently curving arches; newly homogeneous textures; and new methods for achieving formal grandeur." His effortless melodies, sweet but not unctuous harmonies, and sure command of the long line seem like a breath of fresh air when contrasted with the dissonant, convoluted complexities of his medieval predecessors. Loyset Compère (c. 1450–1510) admiringly wrote of Dufay: "Moon of all music; light of singers."

SELECTED RECORDINGS

DUNSTABLE: SACRED AND SECULAR MUSIC
Soloists, Ambrosian Singers; Denis Stevens, conductor
Musical Heritage Society MHS 686

MUSIC OF THE EARLY RENAISSANCE: JOHN DUNSTABLE AND HIS CONTEMPORARIES
The Purcell Consort of Voices, Grayston Burgess, director, with the Musica Reservata of London
Turnabout TV 34058S

DUNSTABLE: FOUR MOTETS; O ROSA BELLA
Purcell Consort of Voices, Grayston Burgess, director, with the Elizabethan Consort of Viols
Argo ZRG 681

MUSIC OF THE HUNDRED YEARS WAR
Musica Reservata of London conducted by John Beckett
Philips 839 753

THE COURT OF BURGUNDY
Early Music Consort of London directed by David Munrow
EMI ASD 3643. (Volume III of the three-record set The Art of Courtly Love, *available either as EMI HMV 86301 or Seraphim SIC-6092.)*
Secular music by Dufay and Binchois

DUFAY: MUSIC FROM THE COURT OF BURGUNDY
Musica Reservata conducted by John Beckett
Philips 6500 085

Neither the music of John Dunstable and his English contemporaries nor that of Dufay and the Burgundian Court has fared particularly well on record—particularly surprising in the case of the former, since the English have otherwise served the works of their Renaissance masters so commendably. Nonetheless the eager listener can make a good start toward the appreciation of this memorable music; the cream of the crop is listed above.

The most comprehensive sampling of Dunstable's music may be found on Stevens's album, the only disc devoted entirely to that composer. The choral singing, if sometimes strained, is unfailingly musical, while the solo singing features the wonderfully expressive countertenor of Russell Oberlin. Also worthy is the Argo disc, which features gorgeous singing by the Purcell Consort, not too obtrusively accompanied by viols, organ, and recorder. Three of the pieces may be heard in different realizations by the Purcell Consort on their inexpensive Turnabout album. This offers a wider choice of English and Burgundian pieces (the second side of the Argo album contains secular music by Josquin), equally well sung, but marred by the annoyingly raucous accompaniments of the Musica Reservata in most of the secular works. Fortunately the Musica Reservata's *Court of Burgundy* and *Hundred Years' War* albums are not quite so badly afflicted. These are in fact well worth acquiring for their always engaging music-making as well as for the interesting selection of works. The instrumental problem rears its ugly head again in an unexpected context, David Munrow's Burgundian disc. Though his Early Music Consort performs with their customary polish and enthusiasm, the reliance on loud wind instruments for accompaniments seems almost perverse in this sophisticated music. Even in such a song as Dufay's *Donnés l'assault à la fortresse* (Storm my sweet lady's defenses) the use of shawm and sackbuts comes as a shock; heavy instrumental underlining is not necessary to get to the point.

DUFAY: FIFTEEN SONGS
Musica Mundana; David Fallows, director
1750 Arch Records 1751; also available on Musical Heritage Society MHS 4557

The most generally satisfying single disc of Dufay's secular music comes from an unlikely source, the tiny 1750 Arch label in Berkeley, California. David Fallows, director of the Musica Mundana, carefully selected the chansons to encompass Dufay's entire career. This care extends to the extremely sensible and convincing performance solutions. Some of the songs are realized entirely vocally (always with one to a part), some with several vocalists and at least one instrumentalist, others with a single singer and nicely varied accompanimental forces. These forces are restricted to recorder, viol, lute, and organetto, all eminently believable. And while the singing is rarely of virtuoso standard, it is thoroughly attuned to the composer's intent. Highly recommended.

DUFAY: COMPLETE SECULAR MUSIC
Medieval Ensemble of London, Peter and Timothy Davies, directors
L'Oiseau-Lyre Florilegium D237 D6 (six discs)

Those not content with a mere sampling of Dufay's secular output are directed to the recent six-disc L'Oiseau-Lyre album of the complete secular music. I have not heard it. But the album has been severely criticized for relying on Heinrich Besseler's notoriously problem-ridden editions, for opting for instrumental accompaniment throughout, for frequently placing string instruments in a range lower than was possible in Dufay's time, and for some strange text underlay decisions. The music-making per se, however, has been highly praised; the singers are all men.

DUNSTABLE: FOUR MOTETS; DUFAY: 5 MOTETS
Pro Cantione Antiqua of London, with the London Cornett and Sackbut Ensemble, Bruno Turner, director
DG Archiv 2533 291

BINCHOIS: 4 MOTETS
Pro Cantione Antiqua of London, Bruno Turner, director
DG Archiv 2533 404. Also includes the Missa "L'Homme Armé" by Busnois

The Pro Cantione Antiqua's Dufay/Dunstable disc headlines their important ten-record series of 15th and 16th-century sacred music under Bruno Turner. Like the other discs in the series, it is stunningly sung by the all-male group, but as with too many of the subsequent volumes the realizations are too often slow, static, lacking in drama, and disfigured by instrumental doubling or substitution for the vocal lines (here the intruding instruments are tenor shawms, trombones, rebecs, and organ). Their largely unaccompanied Binchois/Busnois volume is a must, the best introduction on record to the sacred music of two gifted composers for too long known almost exclusively for secular works.

DUFAY: MISSA "SE LA FACE AY PALE," with Chanson and Instrumental Versions
Early Music Consort of London directed by David Munrow
EMI HMV CSD 3751 or Seraphim S 60267

DUFAY: MISSA "ECCE ANCILLA DOMINI"; 4 MOTETS; 2 CHANSONS
Pomerium Musices, Alexander Blachly, director
Nonesuch 71367 H-71367

Though many Dufay masses have been recorded most of these performances suffer from either amateurish singing or insensitivity of style. Two notable exceptions are the contributions by Munrow and Blachly. Munrow's widely praised rendition of Dufay's best-known Mass not only boasts lovingly shaped and incisive music-making, but contains enormous instructional value, for it includes various versions—vocal and instrumental—of the chanson ("Se la face ay pale") on which Dufay based his work. Munrow takes considerable pains to clarify the various appearances of this cantus firmus through instrumental enforcement, and to point up the contrast between full sections (doubled by cornetts and sackbuts) and duos and trios (occasionally accompanied by viols) by reducing the ensemble from two to one per part. Though I would prefer an unaccompanied performance, Munrow's forces bring the music to such vibrant life that there is no need quibbling. I do, however, question the rationale (other than pedagogic) behind drawing special attention to the cantus firmus—an all-too-common procedure in modern-day performances of Renaissance polyphony. Renaissance composers used these cantus firmi as structural edifices, just as medieval composers did with isorhythm. There is no reason to think that they wished the average listener to be aware of the constructional basis of their music—just the contrary is more likely. Moreover, giving special attention to any one line destroys the equality of parts that is such a characteristic feature of Renaissance sacred polyphony.

No instruments intrude in the performance by Blachly and his Pomerium Musices of Dufay's late Missa *Ecce Ancilla* (unusual in that the chant tenor gets its own text, that of the chant on which it is based). All things considered, this disc is probably the outstanding single introduction to Dufay on record. Blachly provides a generous sampling of Dufay's sacred and secular output, the secular works lightly accompanied, the sacred pieces totally unaccompanied. He even supplies the *Ecce ancilla* chant. The special glory of the album is the singing of the small mixed chorus: their intonation is so flawless that the harmonies actually ring, and the music is shaped with a purpose and acumen sadly missing in most realizations of this repertoire.

8

THE
HIGH
RENAISSANCE

The Netherlands (1450–1550)

As the Middle Ages drew to a close, music was in a state of separatism, mannerism, and confusion. From this disorder Dunstable and Dufay forged a new International style (see chapter 7) that was to serve as a model for well over a century. Because virtually all the important composers writing in this style emanated from what is today central and southern Holland, Belgium, and the northeastern portion of France, they have commonly been labelled Franco-Flemish, and the century 1450–1550 is known as "the age of the Netherlanders." Most of these composers worked for the Emperor, the King of France, the Pope, or at one of the Italian courts (while Italy did not actually produce any major composers during this period, it did provide employment for some of the greatest).

Busnois and Ockeghem

The most significant composers of the generation after Dufay and Binchois were Antoine Busnois (c. 1430–92) and Johannes Ockeghem (c. 1420–97). In many respects their careers paralleled those of their predecessors. Busnois, like Binchois, spent most of his career in the employ of the Burgundian court, and excelled in elegant and refined chansons, often to hedonistic texts of his own creation. But unquestionably the dominant musician of his era, and the successor to Dufay as master of the large-scale form, was Ockeghem.

Ockeghem served for more than 50 years as chaplain, composer, and chapelmaster to the French kings Charles VII, Louis XI, and Charles VIII, and was much honored and highly remunerated during his own lifetime. Though Ockeghem wrote relatively little (12 Masses, 10 motets, and some 20 chansons survive from his hand), what does come down is of extraordinary quality.

Johannes Ockeghem (c. 1420–1497), pictured in the dark glasses with his choir at the chapel of the King of France. Note the small size of this group, its all-male constitution, the large choirbook from which everyone sings, and the lack of instrumental accompaniment.

Where Dufay's music impresses us by its grace, soaring majesty, and formal clarity, Ockeghem presents an entirely different musical personality: moody, flamboyant, enigmatic. In common with so many composers of the era, Ockeghem was trained as a singer. His deep bass voice was greatly admired and may explain his fondness for exploring previously unnavigated subterranean registers. A characteristic aspect of Ockeghem's music is its integration of old medieval techniques of hidden structures into the new contrapuntal Renaissance style. One notable example is the use of canon in his *Missa Prolationum* (Mass of the Time Signatures). Each movement of this four-part piece contains two different canons sung simultaneously, with each part moving at a different speed. No less astonishing are his *Missa Cuiusvis toni* (Mass in any mode) which may be sung in any one of four modes, and the motet *Deo gratias*, a canon for four nine-part choruses (36 total parts). Yet despite the enormous technical feat involved in composing such works, Ockeghem created music of contemplative vastness and inward rapture.

Josquin des Prez

Ockeghem was also revered as a teacher. Among his many students may well have been the incomparable Josquin des Prez (c. 1440–1521), the most esteemed composer of his age. The historian Cosimo Bartoli in 1567 compared Josquin's stature as a musician to Michelangelo's as an artist. As late as 1711 Andrea Adami cited Josquin as the father of contrapuntal music, an unusual tribute for an era when musicians of even the immediately preceding generation were quickly forgotten. It was Josquin who more than any other composer set forth the principles of systematic imitation which were to form the stylistic basis of polyphonic music for the rest of the century. His exquisitely shaped lines, beguiling textures, and carefully ordered harmonies produced a music of surpassing breadth and formal logic, music so carefully articulated that it is surprisingly easy to follow even at its most complex. But the aspect of Josquin's art that fostered such a furor among his contemporaries was its remarkable expressivity: to a far greater extent than anyone before him Josquin attempted to convey the meanings of the words he set. For this reason his most powerful and audacious music is not to be found in his twenty-odd Masses, in which the text remains fixed, but rather in his 100 or so motets, whose texts he could select himself.

For example, the eloquent lament *Absalon, fili mi* (Absalon, my son) concludes with a stunning example of word painting to the text "but go down weeping to the grave." Josquin conveys this image by a sequential descent through the circle of progressively flatter keys. This "progression not only demonstrates the composer's success in exploring the outer limits of musical space," maintains Howard Brown, "but also symbolizes the idea of a descent into hell in an almost physically palpable way."

Josquin des Prez (c. 1440–1521), the most esteemed composer of his age. Even Martin Luther exclaimed: "He is the master of the notes. They must do as he wills; as for the other composers, they have to do as the notes will."

It was undoubtedly brilliant strokes of this sort that moved Martin Luther to exclaim of Josquin: "He is the master of the notes. They must do as he wills; as for the other composers, they have to do as the notes will." But there was another aspect to Josquin's personality. When the Duke Hercules d'Este I of Ferrara sought a composer for his court, his secretary recommended Heinrich Isaac over Josquin, because Isaac "is able to

get on better with his colleagues and composes new pieces
quicker. It is true, Josquin composes better, but he does it only
when it suits him and not when it is requested. More than this,
Josquin asks 200 ducats while Isaac is pleased with 120.'' The
Duke rejected this advice and hired Josquin, who emerges as the
Beethoven of his time, a man who knew his own worth and wrote
what and for whom he pleased. The age of the individual was at
hand.

Contemporaries of Josquin
If Josquin towered above his contemporaries, this does not
devalue their work. For he was surrounded by a host of lesser
luminaries, substantial composers in their own right. Among the
most prominent names were Alexander Agricola (1446–1506),
Jacob Obrecht (c. 1450–1505), Loyset Compère (c. 1450–1518),
Heinrich Isaac (c. 1450–1517), Jean Mouton (c. 1459–1522),
Antoine Brumel (c. 1460–c. 1520), and Pierre de la Rue
(c. 1460–1518). Even now, however, their works are so seldom
performed and recorded that it is difficult to formulate more than
a vague impression of their musical personalities. But it is clear
enough that they were far more than carbon copies of Josquin.
Consider Obrecht, la Rue, and Isaac. Though born after Josquin,
Obrecht was for many years linked with Ockeghem, perhaps due
to his essential conservatism. Obrecht's music lacks the textural
variety, rhythmic animation, and emotional impact of Josquin, or
for that matter the brooding whimsy of Ockeghem's, but it does
possess a forthright vigor, a warmth, and quirky spontaneity that
are immediately likable. La Rue, on the other hand, writes in a
richly textured style full of contrapuntal artifice and sombre
dignity. Heinrich Isaac was perhaps the greatest of Josquin's
contemporaries, even more versatile and cosmopolitan than
Josquin himself, a master of sonorous possibility and emotional
penetration.

High Renaissance Style
One of the great accomplishments of the composers of the High
Renaissance, as Josquin's era has become known, was the
development of systematic principles of imitation. Each phrase of
text would be given its own "point of imitation," repeated in turn
by every voice part before moving on to the next phrase in a
continuously overlapping series. As time went on, the Franco-
Flemish composers grew freer and freer in their imitative procedures, so that the imitative phrases were shorter and less
recognizably drawn from a model, and the various entrances
were less clearly defined. Moreover, the standard number of
parts was expanded from four to five or six. The result was a
denser, more seamless textural fabric.The major exponents of
these techniques were Nicolas Gombert (c. 1500–c. 1556), Jacob
Clemens non Papa (c. 1510–c. 1556/8), and Adrian Willaert
(c. 1490–1562). I list Willaert last, for though he was born before
Gombert and Clemens he outlived them both, and was by a
considerable margin the most progressive of the three. During
his service as chapelmaster at St. Mark's cathedral in Venice
(1527–62) Willaert moved toward a new, "Venetian" style
characterized by natural declamation, sensitive though restrained
expression of the text, chordally oriented counterpoint, and

antiphonal writing for two choirs. In so doing he established the basis for the subsequent achievements of Andrea and Giovanni Gabrieli and for entrance into a new world, that of the Baroque.

"Parody" Technique

The principal method for constructing large-scale pieces during the age of Dufay and Josquin was *cantus firmus* technique, whereby a preexisting tune placed in the tenor (by then that part just above the bass) would serve as the scaffolding for the entire piece. During the 16th century treatment of the cantus firmus became increasingly loose. Instead of quoting a melody literally, composers now more likely than not would *paraphrase* it, changing rhythms and adding or subtracting notes, in effect creating an entirely new melody. Nor need the cantus firmus be confined to a single voice—it might "migrate" from the tenor to another voice part or even appear in two or more parts simultaneously. This latter procedure gives rise to still another: to base a work not on a single melodic line but on two or more parts taken from another piece. Though this new practice, termed *parody*, is a logical extension of the old, it actually introduces a revolutionary concept. Both cantus firmus and paraphrase composition draw from a monophonic model; parody, on the other hand, depends on a polyphonic model. Parody should not be viewed in the derogatory sense of "to make fun of," but rather simply in the sense of "to derive from." Frequently composers would take the entire musical substance of a chanson, motet, mass, or madrigal and rework it to form a piece recognizably their own. As a rule, they transformed a relatively simpler design into one of greater complexity.

Parody technique, which became the standard means of Mass composition by 1540, strikingly reveals the liberal attitude taken by Renaissance composers toward preexisting music. No crime was attached to borrowing from a contemporary; indeed, this was a way of honoring him and at the same time showing off one's own ability by improving upon the work of another. Not until the 19th century did "originality" become the restrictive albatross it has remained for composers today.

SELECTED RECORDINGS

Anthology

THE ART OF THE NETHERLANDS
Early Music Consort of London directed by David Munrow
Available as EMI SLS 5049 or Seraphim SIC-6104 (three discs)
Secular songs, instrumental music, Mass movements, and motets
CHANSONNIER CORDIFORME
The Consort of Musicke directed by Anthony Rooley
L'Oiseau-Lyre Florilegium D186D 4 (four discs)

Early

OCKEGHEM: COMPLETE SECULAR MUSIC
Medieval Ensemble of London
L'Oiseau-Lyre Florilegium D254D 3 (three discs)
OCKEGHEM: "MISSA MA MAISTRESSE"; MISSA "AU TRAVAIL SUIS"; 2 MOTETS; 2 CHANSONS
Pomerium Musices, Alexander Blachly, director
Nonesuch H-71336

OCKEGHEM: MISSA PROLATIONUM; LUPI: MOTET TO
OCKEGHEM'S MEMORY
Musical Heritage Society MHS 4026
OCKEGHEM: 7 MOTETS: BUSNOIS: IN HYDRAULIS
Musical Heritage Society MHS 4179
Capella Nova, Richard Taruskin, director
BUSNOIS: MISSA "L'HOMME ARMÉ"
Pro Cantione Antiqua of London, Bruno Turner, director
DG Archiv 2533 404. Also includes four motets by Binchois
BUSNOIS: 8 CHANSONS
The Nonesuch Consort, Joshua Rifkin, director
Nonesuch H-71247

The greatest scandal of the entire Renaissance discography has
been the continued scarcity of decent performances of Franco-
Flemish sacred polyphony, the very heart of the era's music.
While this situation has improved but slightly in the past decade,
there happily now exists a superb anthology surveying the High
Renaissance. Appropriately entitled *The Art of the Netherlands,* it
comes from a predictable source: David Munrow and his estima-
ble Early Music Consort of London. This was one of the last
projects Munrow completed before his tragic suicide in 1976 at
the age of 33. With his death, the world of early music lost
perhaps its most vital and influential figure. *The Art of the*
Netherlands fully maintains and in some respects even surpasses
Munrow's three other magnificent multi-disc anthologies: *Music*
of the Gothic Era, The Art of Courtly Love, and *Instruments of the*
Middle Ages and Renaissance. Half the album deals with secular
and instrumental music; these selections will in no way disappoint
those expecting Munrow's customary blend of thoroughgoing
scholarship (even the pronunciation was painstakingly prepared),
startling virtuosity, mastery of style, and extraordinary ability to
entertain.

But the true substance of the album lies in the three sides of
Mass movements and motets. The pieces were obviously chosen
with great care, for they are of almost uniformly high quality and,
moreover, tellingly elucidate the wide variety of styles and
techniques exemplified by the Franco-Flemish masters. High-
lights include a Tinctoris *Kyrie* notable for its astonishingly low
tessitura, an incredibly resplendent 12-part *Gloria* by Brumel, a
powerful six-part canonic setting by la Rue of the *Sanctus,* and
Mouton's *Nesciens Mater virgo virum,* a rapt eight-part canonic
motet of overwhelming impact. Munrow seems to have re-
thought performance practice since his *Gothic Era* and *Courtly*
Love albums. He occasionally uses women on the soprano line in
sacred as well as secular works (though this results in a mushier
texture than the all-men ensembles), and—far more
importantly—dispenses entirely with instrumental accompaniment in the sacred pieces. The sheer beauty, purity, and
authority of some of this singing must be heard to be believed.
And I can't imagine anyone hearing this album not wishing to
immediately begin exploring the works of these Franco-Flemish
composers in more detail.

Church choirs during most of the Renaissance generally sang
from large choirbooks placed on a lectern; these books were of
such dimensions that as many as 20 singers could easily read off

them. There are many pictures illustrating such performances, including a famous one of Ockeghem and his chorus of eight. Secular music, on the other hand, was typically rendered from tiny partbooks designed for one (and at the very most three) singers. Most of the surviving repertoire of courtly secular music from the last half of the 15th century comes down through richly illuminated *chansonniers* obviously designed not for daily use but as wealthy collectors' editions. The most lavish of all is the heart-shaped Chansonnier Cordiforme, covered in red velvet. Predictably, the songs deal almost exclusively with courtly love. All told there are some forty-three songs, most of very high quality. Represented are nearly all the major composers writing in the genre at the time of the manuscript's compilation c. 1475, so that in toto this chansonnier provides the most comprehensive single introduction to aristocratic song of the late 15th century. Fortunately for us, it has now been recorded complete, in a production of great care and performances of substantial attainment by Rooley's Consort of Musicke. All that is missing is that special empathy with the music so brilliantly captured in Munrow's anthology.

Busnois fares decently on disc, what with the Pro Cantione Antiqua at their considerable best in his Missa "L'Homme armé" and Joshua Rifkin's attractively planned and unpretentiously realized collection of chansons.

For many years Ockeghem's secular music was hardly available on disc. Now it can be had complete, from the Medieval Ensemble of London, whose musical performances have garnered widespread praise.

The sacred music of Ockeghem was long subjected to murky, tremulous recordings that obscured, even obliterated, the subtleties of his part-writing and the unique personality of individual works. Now, however, his work may be heard in stunning *a capella* realizations by recently formed New York-based groups, Pomerium Musices (Blachly) and Capella Nova (Taruskin). Blachly's Ockeghem disc is every bit as good as his Dufay album. It is intelligently conceived (each Mass is preceded by the chanson on which it was based) and sung with the same technical assurance, awe-inspiring vocal blend, and powerful expressivity. Particularly impressive is the haunting, anguished, kaleidoscopically colorful (and without instruments!) *Missa "Au travail suis"* (I am in torment). Scarcely less valuable are the Ockeghem discs by Richard Taruskin and his Capella Nova, one featuring that canonic tour-de-force, the *Missa Prolationum*, the other six Marian motets. Taruskin, like Blachly, uses female sopranos for the uppermost lines. But where Blachly relies on countertenors for the alto parts, Taruskin uses a blend of male and female altos. The Capella Nova is the larger of the two ensembles: 18–20 singers compared with the Pomerium Musices' 9–12. From them Taruskin elicits readings fuller and less individualized in sonority, broader in tempo and conception, more rough-hewn in timbre, less theatrical in character. I prefer the Blachly approach (and personnel), but why quibble? These are among the finest groups now performing Renaissance polyphony, and both should make more recordings posthaste.

High Renaissance
JOSQUIN: MISSA "L'HOMME ARMÉ" (a sexti toni)
Josquin Choir, Jeremy Noble, director
Vanguard HM 3 SD (with four motets)

JOSQUIN: MISSA "L'HOMME ARMÉ" (super voces musicales)
Pro Cantione Antiqua of London, Bruno Turner, director
DG Archiv 2533 360 (with 2 motets by Josquin and laments on the death of Josquin by Gombert and Vinders)

JOSQUIN: SECULAR MUSIC
Musica Reservata conducted by Andrew Parrott
Argo ZRG 793
Purcell Consort of Voices, Grayston Burgess, director, with the
Elizabethan Consort of Viols
Argo ZRG 681

ISAAC: MISSA "O PRAECLARA"; MOTETS AND CHANSONS
Capella Antiqua of Munich, Konrad Ruhland, director
Telefunken Das Alte Werk SAWT 9544

Considering Josquin's stature, his discographic representation is of pitiful quality. Only two of his Masses get truly adequate performances. Both masses are based, like Busnois', on the secular tune "L'Homme armé," one of the most popular subjects for cantus firmi. Noble's and Turner's approaches make for interesting comparisons. Both are unaccompanied, both are all-men, but Noble's ensemble comprises 18 voices, Turner's 10. Noble's rendition is brisker, more dramatic, conceived on a larger scale; Turner's is clearer in texture, airier, less emotionally involved. The same might be said of the respective motet performances. As one might expect, the music itself is of enormous expressive power.

Similarly fascinating comparisons may be drawn from the two listed discs of Josquin's secular music, both excellent (and, for that matter, from the generous Josquin selection on Munrow's anthology). The Purcell Consort's all-male performances, mostly accompanied by viols, are—like the Dunstable selections on the reverse side—elegant and persuasive. Even better, to my taste, is the Musica Reservata's collection. They eschew loud instruments, yet manage with their distinctive style to infuse Josquin's music with tremendous animation; a stimulating disc.

Isaac has been even more poorly treated on record than Josquin. Probably the most satisfactory all-Isaac album is Ruhland's. His use of instrumental doubling is less annoying than is usually the case (several works are even performed *a cappella)*, and the spirit is right, so that a substantial proportion of the music's beauty shines through.

Late
GOMBERT, CLEMENS, WILLAERT, RORE, MONTE: MOTETS
DG Archiv 2533 321
OBRECHT, LA RUE: MOTETS
DG Archiv 2533 377
Mouton, Isaac, Compère, Brumel: Motets
DG Archiv 2533 378
All with Pro Cantione Antiqua of London, Bruno Turner, director

The most comprehensive selection of motets by Netherlands composers may be found on the three listed volumes from the Pro Cantione Antiqua's Franco-Flemish series. These volumes reveal the group both at its most memorable and its most frustrating. They use no more than two to a part and often sing unaccompanied, which allows the complex polyphony to emerge with maximum clarity and heightens the purely sensuous appeal of the voices. And there is no question about it—Turner boasts a true ensemble of soloists, virtuosos who unabashedly sing virtuosically. Great extremes of dynamics are invoked, as are subtle details of phrasing and rubato. Everything is kept under fastidious control, to be sure, but the constant search for expressivity coupled with prevailingly slow tempos frequently destroys the long line and leads to preciousness. What is missing is the lack of a sure guiding hand, someone who directs everything away from the music-making and toward the music. A comparison between Turner's and Munrow's equally well-sung performances should make this crucial distinction clear.

9

NATIONAL STYLES

The complex imitative polyphony developed by the Franco-Flemish composers may truly be regarded as an international style, for it was practiced throughout Western Europe and in many parts of Eastern Europe as well. A Latin Mass by the German Isaac could fit into a Polish or Spanish service just as easily as into a French or Italian one. It was on such large-scale works that most composers expended their greatest efforts. But concurrent with the writing of this learned counterpoint was the cultivation of idioms and genres peculiar to each country. This music was of course generally in the vernacular, and much of it was simple and tuneful in nature, easily comprehended and easily enjoyed. Such masters as Josquin and Isaac were as adept at these popular pieces as they were at high art.

Germany

In Germany, as noted in Chapter 5, Oswald von Wolkenstein began a tradition of polyphonic lieder which continued unabated into the Renaissance. The earliest examples, mostly anonymous, are housed in three great collections from the second half of the 15th century: the Lochaimer Liederbuch (c. 1455–60), Schedelsches Liederbuch (1460s), and Glogauer Liederbuch (1470s–80s). These song books also contain many monophonic pieces, a tradition continued in the songs of the *Meistersingers*, the most famous of whom was the Nuremberg cobbler Hans Sachs (1494–1576), author of some 6000 songs. As Howard Brown aptly puts it, their guilds were formed of ''self-conscious and pedantic amateur musicians who modeled themselves on the noble medieval Minnesingers.''

Far more important was the extension of the polyphonic lieder tradition in the hands of genuine masters. The most gifted were four figures connected with the court of the Holy Roman

Ludwig Senfl (c. 1486–1542/43), most important pupil of Heinrich Isaac, equally at home in Catholic and Lutheran polyphony as well as in German lied.

Emperor Maximilian I (reigned 1493–1519): Issac, whom we have already encountered, Paul Hofhaimer (1459–1537), Heinrich Finck (1447–1527), and Ludwig Senfl (c. 1486–1542/43). They developed a style of wide scope and deceptive simplicity. However much artifice was involved, its expression was always clear and direct. Their lieder could range from lusty songs to heartfelt love ballads of devastating poignance. The classic example of the latter is Isaac's nostalgic farewell to his master's long-time residence, *Innsbruck, ich muss dich lassen* (Innsbruck, I must leave you). Isaac demonstrates two-and-a-half centuries before Mozart that a simple melody and harmonies could produce a result as profound as the most intricate creations.

Germans seem to have always tempered their more serious side with a delight in good-natured fun. A case in point is the *quodlibet* (''whatever you like''), agglomerations of various songs or song fragments which formed ludicrously incongruous texts while making perfectly good musical sense.

As might be expected, German religious music before Luther differed little in basic language from that of other nations. Many German-born composers made their careers elsewhere. Nor was there much difference between the religious works written by Catholics and Protestants—at least until the second quarter of the 16th century. Among composers of this sacred repertoire, three stand out: Isaac, Senfl, and Thomas Stoltzer (c. 1475–1526). Isaac, who spent most of his career either in Florence or at the court of Maximilian I, wrote some 30 settings of the Mass Ordinary. But his consummate achievement, one comparable to Leonin's *Magnus Liber*, was a cycle of more than 300 motets for the better portion of the church year based on the liturgical texts and chant melodies of the Mass Proper. This monumental work was completed by Senfl, Isaac's foremost pupil. Senfl, whose own music displays a beguiling melodic warmth and lyricism, worked primarily for Maxmilian I and at the Bavarian court in

Munich. Stoltzer is the least known of the triumvirate. Much of his music was written for Queen Mary of Hungary. He emerges as a figure of stubborn integrity whose works are distinguished by tight, angular, endlessly fascinating polyphony, remarkable individuality of line and rhythm, a thoroughgoing command of vocal sonority, and an astonishing gift for simply and eloquently conveying the meaning of his texts.

Spain

Spanish sacred polyphony, too, evinced strong links to the Franco-Flemish idiom. French, Flemish, and German musicians were heavily employed by Spanish courts and cathedrals. And Spain maintained close musical and political ties with Italy: Alfonso V of Aragon became King of Naples in 1442; the first great Spanish Renaissance composer, Christóbal de Morales (c. 1500–53), spent 10 years as a member of the Papal chapel. Spanish religious music tended to balance a conservatism of style with tremendous emotional intensity.

Not only church music but also a notable production of indigenous secular song flourished under the Catholic monarchs Ferdinand of Aragon and Isabella of Castile (married in 1469). These were collected in books called *cancioneros*. As with much of the Renaissance song repertoire, many of the pieces exist both as vocal part-music and as solo songs with instrumental accompaniment. The ideal was not polyphony of equal parts, but rather a single dominant melodic line, usually in the top voice. The principal genre was the *villancico*, a short strophic song with refrain and a fixed repetition scheme (aBccaB). Musically villancicos are typically tuneful works, with the bass supplying a strong harmonic foundation, and inner parts designed more as harmonic enrichers than as distinct melodies. Generally they were either chordal or lightly contrapuntal. The resulting music was simple and direct in spirit, far removed from the International polyphonic style. But villancicos, unlike the light-hearted Italian frottole, which they closely resemble, encompass a surprisingly great variety of subject matter and emotional range—many, indeed, are quite serious. The greatest master of this genre was Juan del Encina (1469–1529). Other important Spanish song composers were Juan Vásquez (c. 1500–c. 1560), who cultivated not only Villancicos but also Italian madrigals, Mateo Flecha the elder (c. 1481–1533) and his nephew and namesake, the younger (c. 1520–1604), noted for their *ensaladas*. An ensalada was not a food, but the Spanish equivalent of the quodlibet.

Spanish secular music nicely complements the sobriety and reverence of its sacred counterpart. Much of this music manifests a noteworthy worldliness. But it is not of the weary-wise variety: these Spaniards reveal that valuable ability to laugh in the face of life's greatest absurdities and cruelest blows—a genuine joy of living.

France

The French, never ones to take life too seriously, made their own special contribution to national genres. This was the Parisian *chanson*. It differed from the learned chanson of such composers as Machaut, Binchois, and Dufay in its chordal style, strongly rhythmic nature, syllabic text settings, and light-hearted, often frivolous subject matter. The principal early masters of the genre were Claudin de Sermisy (c. 1490–1562), notable for his charming melodies, and Clement Jannequin (c. 1485–c. 1560), a student of Josquin who became particularly renowned for his rich output of descriptive or programmatic chansons. These latter were in some respects the Renaissance equivalent of the medieval caccia—not in canonic structure, but in the employment of realistic sounds (of the hunt, birds, battles, city streets, ladies' gossip, etc.) cannily selected for their onomatopoeic potential. Yet for all their entertainment value and sometimes formidable technical wizardry, the Parisian chansons of Claudin, Jannequin, and their contemporaries seldom dig very deep, and their charms pale when heard in other than small doses.

Italy

The same criticism might be levelled at the Italian *frottola,* the earliest and least sophisticated of the genres we have been considering and very likely a model for both the Parisian chanson and the villancico. Frottole were usually strophic and set syllabically to music in four parts. Yet despite the simplicity of these bouncy, tuneful, and harmonically straightforward Italian songs, they should by no means be considered popular art. They were cultivated at the Italian courts, probably in response to the contrapuntal complexities and pretentious texts of the Netherlands chanson. Typical concerns of the frottole were satire and love in its more basic aspects. The most important exponents were Marco Cara (d. c. 1530) and Bartolomeo Tromboncino (d. c. 1535), who murdered his unfaithful wife.

The Madrigal

So seriously limited was the frottola as a vehicle for serious composition that with the deaths of Cara and Tromboncino it more or less passed into oblivion. It was the forerunner, however, of the most important new secular genre of the entire Renaissance, the Italian *madrigal.* This should not be confused with the Trecento madrigal, a strophic song with refrain (see Chapter 5). The new Italian madrigal, like the motet, drew its form from the form of the text—each new phrase of text inspired a new phrase of music. But by this time motets were generally religious pieces in Latin, while madrigals were secular works in the vernacular. The great accomplishment of the madrigal, that which allowed it to become the most progressive form of the late 16th century, was its uniting of learned with simple styles.

Madrigals maintained the Franco-Flemish ideal of equal voice parts, while incorporating the simple choral writing and clear harmonic organization of the frottola. More than any previous genre, madrigals were text-dependent. The vivid description of every detail of the text led to bold experimentation with harmony and texture, and to the wonderfully labile and spontaneous character of these pieces—as the poetry shifted mood, so did the music. Because the ultimate goal of madrigals was the reflection and intensification of the poetry they set, composers assiduously sought out texts worthy of their music (just the opposite of the situation in 14th-century Italy). Probably at no time in history was there such a demand by musicians for high-quality poetry. The result was positive for both sides. Music permitted far more precise control over rhythm and pitch than poetry, and, more-over, could point up multiple meanings through rapid shifts in texture, harmony, and melodic contour—even through the simultaneous presentation of very different melodic (and textual) lines. No wonder Italian madrigals became the preeminent secular musical form of the Renaissance, brilliantly cultivated even by such non-Italians as the Spaniard Juan Vásquez (c. 1500–c. 1560), German Heinrich Schütz (1585–1672), and many, many Netherlanders.

Indeed, with the exception of Costanzo Festa (d. 1545), the most important of those composers who led the madrigal from a frottola-like idiom to one far more flexible and expressive were not Italians. These include Philippe Verdelot (c. 1480–1545), Jacob Arcadelt (c. 1505–60), and Willaert. The greatest madrigalist of the next generation, and the one who did the most to establish the standard use of five-part settings of serious poetry of high literary quality, was Cipriano de Rore (1516–65). Rore was a Netherlander who worked in Italy, studied with Willaert, and for a short period succeeded his teacher as music director at St. Mark's. He excelled at evoking the most minute subtleties of his texts and so paved the way for the virtuoso madrigalists at the end of the century and beyond. But unlike these later madrigalists, Rore was careful not to let local pictorial considerations override the broader musical framework. Among Rore's more distinguished contemporaries writing madrigals were Nicola Vicentino (1511–72), notable especially for his harmonic audacities, and Andrea Gabrieli (1510/20–86), better known for his instrumental music and grand polychoral motets.

Italian music also had its deliberately popular side. Carnival time before Lent in 15th-century Florence featured masked musicians singing *canti carnascialeschi*, strophic satirical songs of a tuneful, mostly choral nature. Isaac and Agricola were the best-known composers. *Villanelle*, lively three-part strophic homophonic settings of unsophisticated, often irreverent verse, thrived around the area of Naples beginning c. 1540. Thomas Morley described them "as clownish music to a clownish matter." By the end of the century the most important light forms were the *canzonetta* ("little song") and the *balletto* ("little dance"), the latter distinguished by its ubiquitous fa-la-la refrains. The principal composer in both these sprightly forms was Giovanni Gastoldi (d. 1622).

England

More so than any European nation, England went its own musical way. The court of Henry VIII (reigned 1509–47) inspired a corpus of vernacular songs and carols. The principal composers were William Cornysh the Younger (c. 1465–1523), Robert Fayrfax (c. 1464–1521), and the King himself, certainly the most notable amateur composer of the age. But this secular repertoire, while delightful is rather slight. Not until the end of the 16th century did the English achieve a truly significant secular style.

Meanwhile most of the serious music was being written for the Church. Curiously, though Power and Dunstable had been instrumental in the development of Dufay's style and the consequent international Franco-Flemish idiom, the Franco-Flemish innovations—perhaps due to England's insular location—had little effect on English composers of the second half of the 15th century. This is to our benefit, for the English, deprived of interaction with the Continent, were forced to develop their own distinctive style. Their accomplishment during this period can best be viewed from the pages of that grand collection of Church music known as the Eton Choirbook, copied c. 1490–1502. Among the major figures represented therein are John Browne, Richard Davy, Walter Lambe and Robert Wylkynson, as well as Cornysh and Fayrfax. Their music, though conservative in technique, tends to be exceedingly dense and complex in texture. Six, even eight parts of highly ornate non-imitative polyphony were not uncommon, and coupled with the luxuriant harmonies, the total effect is one of immense sumptuousness. This style was continued in the music of the next generation, men such as John Redford, Nicolas Ludford, and the Scottish composers Robert Carver and Robert Johnson.

But the greatest of the British composers in the first half of the 16th century was John Taverner (c. 1495–1545). Taverner manages to retain the florid melismatic lines and opulent harmonies of his predecessors while adding a greater variety of texture, more systematic imitation, and more careful large-scale structuring. One of his most famous works is the Mass *The Western Wind*, which, together with the later settings by Tye and Sheppard, comprise the only English Masses known to be based on secular melodies. These three Masses are also unusual in that they treat the cantus firmus as a gigantic series of variations.

In 1539–40 Henry VIII succeeded in confiscating all the monasteries in England (Taverner himself assisted in this process). Yet though thousands of choristers were thrown out of the friaries and monastaries, the effect upon England's musical life hardly proved disastrous. In fact, many church musicians helped contribute—despite uncertain conditions—to a new burgeoning of Latin religious music in England, and just as powerfully to the subsequent flowering of secular music under the reigns of Elizabeth I (1558–1603) and James I (1603–25).

The leading Church composers of the mid-16th century were Christopher Tye (c. 1500–73), John Sheppard (c. 1520/25–63), Robert Whyte, (c. 1530–74), and above all Thomas Tallis (c. 1505–85). Tallis forged a style less abstract and more closely reflective of the text. Among his most memorable pieces are two settings of the *Lamentations of Jeremiah*, music of unforced eloquence, and that astounding contrapuntal *tour de force Spem in alium,* for 40 different voice parts separated into eight five-part choirs.

SELECTED RECORDINGS

Up to this point my selection of recordings was radically circumscribed by scarcity of choice and limited adequacy of performance. For the last three chapters, the situation changes dramatically. Nearly every byway of nationalistic, instrumental, and late Renaissance music—with the glaring exception of the virtuoso Italian madrigal—has been explored on disc in felicitous quality and quantity. So wide is the choice, in fact, that I can only provide a starting point for the beginning collector. I have singled out with an asterisk those discs that are special favorites; these, I

feel, make ideal introductions to this inexhaustible rich repertoire. So high is the general level of musical attainment on most
of the listed discs that detailed analysis seems unnecessary.
Enjoy the records and form your own opinions.

Anthologies

MUSICKE OF SUNDRIE KINDES
The Consort of Musicke directed by Anthony Rooley
L'Oiseau-Lyre Florilegium 12 BB 203-6 (four discs)
*THE PLEASURES OF THE ROYAL COURTS
The Early Music Consort of London; David Munrow, director
Nonesuch H-71326
EARLY MUSIC IN ITALY, FRANCE AND BURGUNDY
Studio der Frühen Musik
Telefunken Das Alte Werk SAWT 9466
*THE KING'S SINGERS' CONTINENTAL COLLECTION
Moss Music Group MMG 1103 or EMI ASD 3557
21 German and Spanish part-songs
THE KING'S SINGERS' MADRIGAL COLLECTION
Moss Music Group MMG 1105 or EMI CSD 3756
21 Italian and English madrigals
THE KING'S SINGERS' A FRENCH COLLECTION
*Moss Music Group MMG 1104 or EMI CSD 3740. 11 French chansons
all with The King's Singers*
RENAISSANCE VOCAL MUSIC
Assorted German groups sing 22 English and Italian madrigals,
French chansons, and German lieder
Nonesuch H-71097

One could hardly imagine a more comprehensive overview of the
astonishing range of Renaissance national styles than the Consort
of Musicke's four-disc set *Music of Sundrie Kindes*. On it can be
found nearly every sort of secular music written by Renaissance
composers c. 1480–1620. There are Franco-Flemish works,
Italian frottole and popular songs, Parisian chansons, German
lieder and Spanish songs as well as *quodlibets* and *ensaladas*,
Italian madrigals and instrumental works, English songs and
instrumental pieces, and even a taste of the early Baroque. And
the selection is laudably unhackneyed. Naturally, not every
performance is of the same quality, but the overall level is high.

Those desiring a more restricted sampling of this repertoire
can turn to a number of superb anthologies. David Munrow
works his familiar magic in *The Pleasures of the Royal Courts*, a
totally captivating survey of the music being written at the courts
of Philip the Good, Emperor Maximilian I, the Medicis (including
three carnival songs), and Ferdinand and Isabella, with a lovely
selection of trouvère songs thrown in for good measure. For my
money, this is the most irresistible of all single-disc early music
anthologies. Scarcely less entertaining is the Studio der Frühen
Musik's album, which concentrates on a lighter repertoire.
Included are music of the Italian Trecento, bird-call vilrelais c.
1400, Burgundian chansons, Parisian theater songs c. 1500, and
Italian music from around 1550. Andrea von Ramm appears at
her virtuosic best.

The King's Singers have nothing to do with a King. Rather,
they are six men who met while students at King's College,

Cambridge. These phenomenal musicians combine full-throated vigor with elegant technique in music-making of enormous flexibility that miraculously manages to avoid indulgences of every sort. Their collections of German and Spanish part-songs, English and Italian madrigals, and French chansons are unrivalled either in selection or presentation. The EMI pressings are far superior to those on the Moss Music Group label. Nonesuch's *Renaissance Vocal Music* album provides an instructive companion to those of the one-to-a-part King's Singers, for it shows how effective the secular part-song literature can be when sung by large mixed ensembles with as much spirit and sensitivity as four different German groups exhibit here.

Germany

STOLTZER: FOUR GERMAN PSALMS; MISSA "DUPLEX PER TOTUM ANNUM"; MOTETS AND SECULAR MUSIC
The Capella Antiqua of Munich conducted by Konrad Ruhland
ABC Seon ABCL-67003/2 (2 discs)
LUDWIG SENFL: COMPOSER TO THE COURT AND CHAPEL OF EMPEROR MAXIMILIAN I
Missa Paschalis (Easter Mass); sacred and secular selections. New York Pro Musica; Noah Greenberg, director
American Decca DL 79420
*MUSIC FOR MAXIMILIAN: SOUNDS OF THE RENAISSANCE AT THE COURT OF THE HOLY ROMAN EMPIRE
Assorted soloists; RIAS Chamber Choir, Günther Arndt, conductor
Angel 36379 or Odeon C 91107
TRIUMPH OF MAXIMILIAN I
Early Music Consort of London under David Munrow
British Decca SA6 or London Stereo Treasury STS 15555
GERMAN SONGS OF THE MIDDLE AGES AND THE RENAISSANCE
Hugues Cuenod, tenor; Hermann Leeb, lute
Westminster W-9621. 18 selections
LIEDER AND DANCES FROM GERMANY 1460–1560
Assorted soloists; Capella Lipsiensis directed by Dietrich Knothe
DG Archiv 2533 066
*PEASANT, DANCE, AND STREET SONGS IN GERMANY
C. 1490–1540
Studio der Frühen Musik
Telefunken Das Alte Werk SAWT 9486

Thus far in this survey, the finest performances have largely emanated from a handful of internationally recognized early music groups, primarily from the UK or US. Many of these same groups have produced outstanding contributions in the repertoire now under consideration. A striking case in point is the Studio der Frühen Musik's anthology of humorous and bucolic German songs from the early 16th century, a foot-tapping collection of tunes that should cure any case of mild depression. Not all the music is of the sprightly variety: Senfl's *Ich stund an einem morgen* and especially Stoltzer's *Entlawbet ist der Walde* are songs of the utmost poignance, glowingly sung by Nigel Rogers.

But one of the special joys of listening to nationalistic works on record is the discovery of outstanding native artists who bring a special quality of identification and tonal rightness to the music of their country. Such a disc is *Music for Maximilian*. This all-German production features that late great tenor Fritz Wunderlich in his prime, and encompasses a broad variety of performance styles, including four renditions of *Innsbruck, ich muss dich lassen*. If the realizations vary in quality, the whole is so compelling and magnificently recorded that cavils are quickly dispelled. My other Germanic selections are similarly satisfying.

A refreshing contrast to the busy and raucous instrumental accompaniments so many modern performers love to provide for the medieval and Renaissance song literature is Hugues Cuenod's German collection, simply and eloquently sung to lute accompaniment (or no accompaniment whatsoever).

Spain and Portugal

WELTLICHE MUSIK IM CHRISTLICHEN UND JÜDISCHEN SPANIEN 1450–1550
Ensemble Hespèrion XX
EMI Reflexe 1C 163-40 125/26 (two discs) or EMI Reflexe 1C 063 30930

SONGS AND DANCES OF CERVANTES' TIME (1547–1616)
Ensemble Hespèrion XX conducted by Jordi Savall
Peters International PLE 051

MUSIC FROM THE COURT OF FERDINAND AND ISABELLA
The Early Music Consort of London conducted by David Munrow
Angel S-36926 or EMI CSD 3738

MUSIC FROM THE TIME OF CHRISTOPHER COLUMBUS
Musica Reservata conducted by John Beckett
Philips 839 714

*THE SONGBOOK OF THE DUKE OF CALABRIA (Upsala Songbook)
Madrid Madrigal Quartet; Lola Rodriguez Aragón, director
Musical Heritage Society MHS 1946

HISPANIAE MUSICAE: ANTHOLOGY OF 16TH-CENTURY VOCAL PART-MUSIC
Quartet Polifonic de Barcelona directed by Miquel Querol
DG Archiv 198 454

SECULAR SPANISH MUSIC OF THE SIXTEENTH CENTURY
The Ambrosian Consort; Denis Stevens, director. Roy Jessen, harpsichord
Oryx 717

SPANISH SONG OF THE RENAISSANCE 1440–1600
Victoria de los Angeles, voice; Ars Musicae Ensemble of Barcelona directed by José M. Lamaña
Seraphim S-60349

CANCIONES ESPAÑOLAS: SONGS FROM THE MIDDLE AGES AND RENAISSANCE
Teresa Berganza, mezzo-soprano; Narciso Yepes, guitar
DG 2530 504

MORALES: MAGNIFICAT: 5 MOTETS
Pro Cantione Antiqua of London directed by Bruce Turner
DG Archiv 2533 321

Spanish performers have served their secular Renaissance music exceptionally well. The best place to experience their accomplishment is through the extensive Hispavox History of Spanish

Music series, available through Musical Heritage Society. Volume XV, *The Songbook of the Duke of Calabria (1556)*, may well be the prize of the group. From this songbook, the first printed in Spain, has been assembled an incredibly varied group of 23 mostly anonymous villancicos. The singing cannot be too highly praised: this unaccompanied mixed quartet captures every mood and detail of these vibrant songs; the characteristic Spanish vibrato imparts a pleasantly earthy quality. This is the real thing. And the production is stunning all around, with an enormously informative 12-page booklet by Robert Pla.

Querol's mixed Barcelona ensemble, though not so extravagantly talented as the Madrid group, furnishes flavorful and authentic performances encompassing a far larger repertoire. Indeed one could hardly wish a better-chosen succinct overview of Spanish sacred and secular vocal music of the 16th century. If the Barcelonians' unaccompanied singing tends to be a trifle sober, ready compensation comes in the guise of the tremendously invigorating Spanish collections from the Musica Reservata. Their robust style is most appropriate to the more extroverted repertoire (vocal and instrumental); the more delicate pieces are better handled on Stevens' very satisfying disc. Munrow and confreres do equally well on both counts. The occasional duplications between these albums make for engaging comparisons.

Just as worthy of acquisition are the albums by the Ensemble Hespèrion XX. Ensemble Hespèrion XX is something of a Spanish equivalent of the Early Music Quartet, a group comprised largely of instrumentalists (the dazzling Montserrat Figueras is the only vocalist), which should tell you something about their orientation. Their approach is surprisingly subtle yet adventurous, with plenty of improvisation. They are stimulating.

Rarely do international operatic singers venture into the world of Renaissance music. Memorable exceptions are those albums by Victoria de los Angeles and Teresa Berganza. They sing with great beauty of tone and heartfelt intensity, if with a considerably different type of voice (bigger and more sensuous, but not necessarily more appropriate) than customary.

France

*THE RONSARD CIRCLE. PIERRE DE RONSARD: RENAISSANCE SETTINGS OF HIS POETRY
Stéphane Caillat Vocal Quartet and assisting instrumentalists directed by Stéphane Caillat
Musical Heritage Society MHS 1994

*LA CHANSON & LA DANSE: PARIS C. 1540
Soloists of the Vocal Ensemble of Lausanne; Michel Corboz, conductor. Ricercare, Ensemble of Renaissance Instruments, Zurich; Michel Piguet, conductor
Musical Heritage Society MHS 1125

AIRS DE COUR ET CHANSONS SATIRIQUES
Ars Antiqua de Paris
Inedits RTF 995 033

AIRS DE COUR: DRINKING SONGS FROM THE REIGN OF LOUIS XIII
Nigel Rogers, tenor; Anthony Bailes, lute
Peters International PLE-050

The French too have produced several notable recordings of their country's Renaissance music. Particularly striking are the chanson collections from the Vocal Ensemble of Lausanne and Ars Antiqua of Paris, pungent and vividly characterized along the lines of the Musica Reservata, but with an utterly French flavor. Of the two, the MHS disc would be my first choice, because of its instructive grouping of vocal chansons with instrumental arrangements of them and because of the use of unequal temperament for the keyboard instruments. Equal temperament, the tuning system most common today, allows music to sound just as well in any key. In unequal temperament those keys with many sharps and flats are badly out of tune, but the simpler keys generally used are purer in intonation than any in the later equal-tempered system. Moreover; every key in the unequal (mean-tone) system possesses a distinct character of its own, since its tuning is not quite like any other. This explains why Renaissance and Baroque composers claimed different affects for, say, the keys of F and D. All Renaissance keyboard instruments were customarily tuned according to some type of unequal temperament; equal temperament did not come into its own until the late Baroque, Bach's *Well-Tempered Clavier* being the foremost example.

Another French recording of equal merit is the Stéphane Caillat Vocal Quartet's selection of 20 settings by 12 composers of texts by Pierre de Ronsard (1524–85), perhaps the most frequently set poet of the entire 16th century. Included are not only chansons of considerable sophistication, but also tuneful, often monophonic songs known as *vaux-de-vire* or *voix-de-ville* (voice of the town) and later *air de cour*. These, wrote one Renaissance wit, were meant to "be sung or whistled on the streets." An informative booklet accompanies this disc. The singing of the mixed ensemble is sympathetic and distinctively French—no one could mistake the attractively nasal tone quality and idiomatic pronunciation as anything but.

Italy

GASTOLDI/RORE: SECULAR VOCAL MUSIC
Les Menestrals Savoyards; Michel Dubois, director
Musical Heritage Society MHS 1930
VINCENTINO: VOCAL AND INSTRUMENTAL MUSIC
The Jaye Consort of Viols; Francis Baines, director. Accademia
Monteverdiana Consort; Denis Stevens, director
Vanguard Bach Guild HM 34 SD
*PETRUCCI, FIRST PRINTER OF MUSIC:
New York Pro Musica; John Reeves White, director
MCA 2503. Also includes Josquin's Missa Ave Maris Stella
Laude of the 15th and 16th Centuries. Niederaltaich Scholars directed by
Konrad Ruhland. RCA RL 30376

Italy, often called the most musical of all nations, has the dubious distinction of being the only country not to have made outstanding recordings of their own Renaissance music (at least not to my knowledge). For that matter, the Italian madrigal has not fared particularly well on discs from any nation. Denis Stevens and his Ambrosian Consort have probably done more than anyone to explore individual composers. Their Vicentino disc is a real find: serious, sober music of great intensity and harmonic daring. As usual with Stevens' groups, the realizations are musical, well sung, unmannered, and scholarly; they rarely call attention to themselves. The finest available general Italian madrigal collection is that by the King's Singers. Les Menestrals Savoyards perform their Gastoldi/Rore group with becoming spirit, though the sopranos, while not unpleasent, stick out more than I would prefer. Last but hardly least is the New York Pro Musica's selection of chansons, frottole, and popular Italian dances from the earliest printed music books. Some might quibble today with the lavish use of instruments on this venerable disc, but only the most insensitive soul could fault their musicality. Performances such as those of the lauda *Se mai per maraveglia* and frottola *Lirum bililirum* remain true classics.

England

LOVE, LUST, PIETY AND POLITICS: MUSIC OF THE ENGLISH COURT FROM KING HENRY V TO KING HENRY VIII
Pro Cantione Antiqua and Early Music Consort of London directed by Bruno Turner
Harmonia Mundi BASF 25 22286-1 or Quintessence 7185
*TO ENTERTAIN A KING: MUSIC FOR HENRY VIII AND HIS COURT
Musica Reservata directed by Michael Morrow; Purcell Consort of Voices directed by Grayston Burgess
Argo ZK 24
*ETON CHOIRBOOK
Sacred Music by Lambe, Browne, Nesbett, Wylkynson, Cornysh, and Fawkyner. The Purcell Consort of Voices and Choristers of All Saints, Margaret Street, directed by Grayston Burgess
Argo ZRG 557
THE GOLDEN AGE OF ENGLISH SACRED CHORAL MUSIC:
Works by Lambe, Cornyshe, Tallis, and White *(Lamentations of Jeremiah)*. The Scholars
Musical Heritage Society MHS 4441 or Arion ARN 31939
*TAVERNER: "WESTERN WIND" MASS; 4 OTHER SACRED WORKS
King's College Choir; David Willcocks, director
Argo ZRG 5316
TAVERNER: "WESTERN WIND" MASS; MATER CHRISTI. TALLIS: VOTIVE ANTIPHONS, MOTETS AND RESPONDS
The Choir of New College, Oxford; Edward Higginbottom, director
Vanguard Bach Guild HM 78 SD or CRD 1072
TYE: "WESTERN WIND" MASS; "EUGE BONE" MASS
King's College Choir; David Willcocks, director
Argo ZRG 740
SHEPPARD: "WESTERN WIND" MASS; TALLIS: "SALVE INTEMERATA VIRGO" MASS
St. John's College Choir; George Guest, director
EMI ASV DCA 511
*TALLIS: "SPEM IN ALIUM," THE "LAMENTATIONS OF JEREMIAH," AND OTHER CHURCH MUSIC
King's College Choir and Cambridge University Musical Society Chorus directed by David Willcocks
Argo ZK 30/31 (two discs)

*TALLIS: LAMENTATIONS OF JEREMIAH
The King's Singers (with six motets by Byrd)
Moss Music Group 1107 or EMI HSV CSD 3779
Pro Cantione Antiqua directed by Bruno Turner (with Byrd's Mass
for 3 voices)
DG Archiv 2533 113

To a far greater extent than any other nation England has served
its Renaissance musical heritage superbly well. Not only have
they recorded their music in far greater quantity than any other
nation, but they have done so in performances of dependable
achievement. Indeed, the chances are that *any* British performance of British Renaissance music you find (especially on the
Argo and L'Oiseau-Lyre labels) will be of high quality.

There are two fine collections of music from the British royal
courts. The Pro Cantione's is vocally oriented and traverses a
wider chronological range, while the Purcell Consort liberally
shares the limelight with an instrumental ensemble from the
Musica Reservata (they contribute 14 instrumental selections).
I'd hate to be without either, though overfull arrangements with
hyperactive percussion interfere with the impact of the Pro
Cantione disc. All the singers, incidentally, are male. The music
is by turns pleasingly peppery and touchingly gentle.

Of all the European nations only England has maintained the
Renaissance tradition of superior all-male choruses with male
altos and boy sopranos. As a result England has achieved a
decided edge over other countries in fostering choirs whose
balance and purity of tone ideally suits the bulk of the Renaissance sacred polyphonic literature. With such ensembles, the
music is allowed to eloquently speak for itself. Though the British
choirs have largely neglected the Franco-Flemish repertoire,
they have provided some of the greatest recordings of English
Church music and of sacred polyphony from the late Renaissance
(especially Victoria and Palestrina). I have listed many of the
most notable here and in Chapter 11.

There is no need to describe the sound of particular groups,
for all those listed have mastered that ethereal timbre and clarity
of line so right for this music. Nor is there any need to detail the
qualities of specific performances, for all are on a very high level.
The principal differences from one performance to another lie in
the degree of overt expressivity sought by the conductor.
Burgess, for instance, tends to be more fervent than Willcocks
or Higgenbottom, though this should hardly imply a lack of
passion on the latters' parts.

This "choral" repertoire can also be extremely effective
sung one to a part, as so strikingly demonstrated by the recordings of the all-male Scholars and the King's Singers. The latter
group has produced my favorite version of one of the most-
recorded of all large-scale Renaissance works, Tallis' pair of
Lamentations of Jeremiah. Endlessly rewarding comparisons can
be made between the highly flexible but never exaggerated
King's Singers reading, the superbly colored Willcocks/King's
College Choir rendition, and the almost willfully dramatic Pro
Cantione Antiqua interpretation, gloriously sung all.

10

THE EMANCIPATION OF INSTRUMENTS

It is clear that the Renaissance was primarily a vocal age. Almost all purely instrumental music of the Renaissance had its origin in vocal models. Yet composers gradually evolved styles designed specifically for instruments and their unique capabilities: ensemble music, stylized dance music, solo pieces for keyboard and lute. This emancipation of instruments from their role as accompaniments for voices on the one hand and from the function of pure entertainment (such as a background for dancing or dining) on the other was in fact one of the most important achievements of the Renaissance. Without it, the piano sonatas or string quartets of Beethoven would not exist.

The newfound eminence of instruments reveals itself in the sudden appearance of books on instruments (Sebastian Virdung's *Musica getuscht* of 1511 was the first) and numerous tutors for those wishing to learn to play them, as well as in the phenomenal growth in the number and variety of instruments built. The emergence of polyphonic vocal music with written-out parts suitable for instruments demanded a new class of professional instrumentalist, one who could read music. And so, while most of the great Renaissance composers were still singers, many achieved their fame on one or another instrument: Milán on vihuela, Dowland on lute, Ortiz on viol, Hofhaimer, Byrd, and Cabezón on organ, Bull on harpsichord.

The untutored minstrels also elevated their position by forming guilds and going to work for towns and cities. Virtually every municipality maintained a group of instrumental musicians to provide entertainment at civic ceremonies, holidays, and various other social functions. In Germany the town musicians were termed *Stadtpfeiffer* (town pipers), in Italy *piffari*, in England *waits*. The backbone of such groups was generally the winds, though stringed instruments too would often be admitted. As in the Middle Ages, these instrumentalists still were mostly musically illiterate—they learned their craft in strict secrecy from the time-honored custom of oral transmission from master to pupil. That of course explains why so little of their music survives.

Printed collections of motets and chansons, particularly after about 1540, often contain some sort of indication that such music was suitable for voices *or* instruments. This did not mean that the music was conceived for instruments. Rather, it was a publisher's ploy to increase the potential market for their product. It suggests, however, the existence of a sizable group of instrumentalists searching for appropriate music to play. Naturally publishers found it easier and more profitable to issue vocal music that could readily be played on instruments than to print separate pieces for singers and players. Such collections may account for the Renaissance penchant for homogeneous families of instruments—shawms, krummhorns, trombones, recorders, and many others were available in graded sizes from the tiniest sopranino to elephantine sub-bass. These homogeneous consorts were ideally suited for polyphonic music based on equality of parts, as the vast literature of viol and recorder consort music attests.

Even music designed for a specific instrument often would be derived wholesale from vocal pieces. Such a process was termed *intabulation.* Masses, motets, or secular pieces provided models. From them the instrumentalist tried to retain as much of the polyphonic fabric as possible, while enriching it with embellishments and figurations peculiar to the instrument in question. The true art lay not in mere transferral from a vocal medium to an instrumental one, but in transforming the preexistent material into something idiomatic for that instrument. Eventually vocal models were dispensed with entirely and a genuinely instrumentally conceived idiom was established.

Instrumental Genres

Among the earliest genres of instrumental pieces were the imitative *ricercar* and *canzona,* counterparts respectively of the motet and chanson. These served both for solo and ensemble music. There were in addition more rhapsodic, improvisatory forms going under such names as preludes, toccatas, fantasias, and intonations. Improvisatory pieces are naturally most appropriate for soloists and allow for considerable departure from any vocal models. One important new form that seems to have been entirely instrumental in origin was the theme and variations. This was first cultivated in quantity by the Spanish viheulists and organists, foremost among them the blind Antonio de Cabezón (1510–66), organist for the courts of Charles V and Philip II. However, variation techniques had been practiced long before Cabezón's time in dance music. One type of courtly dance popular toward the turn of the 16th century, the *basse dance,* was actually built on improvisatory techniques: the players extemporized a counterpoint or counterpoints above a preexistent cantus firmus. Such contrapuntal extemporization, most suitable in light-textured music, was one of the two major means of improvisation during the Renaissance; the other, appropriate even in densely contrapuntal pieces (vocal or instrumental), was the embellishment of a given melodic line. Mastery of both sorts of ornamenting was expected of musicians and practiced widely.

Vihuela and Lute

A book of this size can do little more than mention some of the principal Renaissance composers of instrumental music. The lute was far and away the most popular plucked instrument of the Renaissance, having by the 16th century supplanted the harp in supremacy as the instrument *par excellence* for the noble amateur. The Spanish equivalents were the vihuela and guitar; the latter, being easier to play, served as a folk instrument, while the vihuela was the instrument for the virtuoso and courtly society. But by 1600 the vihuela, whose use had always been almost entirely restricted to Spain and Southern Italy, was replaced even in art music by the guitar. By this time the guitar had achieved enormous popularity throughout Europe, surpassing even the lute.

Almost all the important surviving vihuela music appears in seven great *tablatures* (a system of notation which showed not the pitches, but the place at which the strings had to be stopped to produce the requisite pitch), each by a different composer: Luis de Milán (1536), Luis de Narváez (1538), Alonso Mudarra (1546), Enriquez de Valderrábano (1547), Diego Pisador (1552), Miguel de Fuenllana (1554), and Esteban Daza (1576). Among the principal lutenist-composers were the Italian Francesco da Milano (1497–1543), dubbed "il divino" by his contemporaries; the Transylvanian virtuoso Valentin Bakfark (1507–76), lutenist to the King of Hungary; the Mantuan Albert de Rippe (c. 1480–1551), who spent most of his career serving Francis I of France; and in England Thomas Robinson, Francis Cutting, Alfonso Ferrabosco II, and that greatest of all, John Dowland (1562–1626). The key to the pronunciation of his last name and to the character of his music may be drawn from the well-known epithet "semper dolens, semper Dowland."

Such lutenists as Milán and Dowland also composed solo songs in which virtuoso accompanimental parts were provided for the lutenist. In such music it is misleading to even speak of accompaniment, for the lute parts often were elevated to a level equal to those of the singer. Led by Dowland, the British brought the lute song to its highest development. These pieces, termed *ayres,* could be performed in one of two ways: as solo songs with instrumental accompaniment, generally by lute with bass viol on the lowest line; or by voices on all the parts, with or without instrumental support. Besides Dowland, the major composers included Thomas Campion (1567–1620), equally renowned as poet (Dowland too was highly praised for his poetry), Michael Cavendish, Philip Rosseter, Robert Jones, and John Danyel. Their best ayres, particularly those by Dowland, are among the greatest treasures of the Renaissance—music of surpassing intimacy and poignancy. Dowland's *Flow my tears* is a deservedly famous example.

Consort Music

The lute song proved so successful that composers uncomfortable writing lute music substituted a consort of viols for the lute. The leading masters of such *consort songs* were William Byrd (1543–1623) and Orlando Gibbons (1583–1625), along with Dowland the foremost figures of the late Renaissance in England. In these pieces as much interest lies in the instrumental parts as

Orlando Gibbons (1583–1625); one of the foremost figures of the late English Renaissance, equally accomplished as a composer of keyboard and consort music, anthems and madrigals.

in the solo line; indeed, a relatively straightforward vocal melody often movingly contrasts with intricate instrumental counterpoint.

Many consort songs had instrumental parts that easily could stand by themselves. A number of British composers cultivated precisely this sort of purely instrumental consort piece. Though a viol consort was the classic group, these pieces could be for any homogeneous instrumental ensemble, recorders being the next most common. Among the chief exponents of such ensemble music, which often went under such titles as fancy or fantasia, were Tye, Byrd, Dowland, Tomkins, Morley, Alfonso Ferrabosco II, Henry and William Lawes, Matthew Locke, and above all Orlando Gibbons.

These homogeneous ensembles were known as "whole" consorts. The British also cultivated a brand of ensemble music for "broken" consort, that is, consorts with a variety of different types of instruments. Many of these pieces actually specified the instruments to be used, a novelty in the Renaissance period. The first printed book of ensemble music in England was Morley's *First Book of Consort Lessons* (1599), scored for both treble and bass viols, cittern and pandora (both plucked instruments), lute, and recorder. Other famous collections were Rosseter's *Lessons for Consort: Made by sundry Excellent Authors* (1609) for the same forces as the Morley pieces (this was a standard broken consort), John Adson's *Courtly Masquing Ayres Composed to 5. and 6. Parts, for Violins, Consorts and Cornets* [cornettos or zinks] (1621), and the most famous and profound of all, John Dowland's *Lachrimae or Seaven Teares figured in Seaven Passionate Pavans, with divers other Pavans, Galiards, and Almands* (1605) for five viols and lute. Though generally classified as a broken consort, Dowland's *Lachrimae* really amounts to a work for viol consort with lute continuo—the lute part does not emerge as an independent line, but rather reinforces the viols and acts as a coloristic foil, two very Baroque functions.

Viols were not used exclusively in consort; they also accumulated a substantial virtuoso solo literature (sometimes with keyboard accompaniment). The best of it was written by the Spanish gambist Diego Ortiz (c. 1525–c. 1620), whose *Tratado de glosas sobre clausulas* . . . (Rome, 1553) provides the basics of improvisatory technique, and by the English composers headed by Tobias Hume.

Keyboard Music: Germany, Italy, and France

But easily the largest category of solo music was that for keyboard. The principal instruments were harpsichord, organ, virginal, and clavichord. Germany took the early lead, with a circle revolving around the blind organists Conrad Paumann (c. 1410–73) and Paul Hofhaimer (1459–1537), the latter court organist to Maximilian I. From the 250-odd pieces in the *Buxheimer Orgelbuch* (c. 1450), the 14 in Arnolt Schlick's *Tabulaturen* (1512), and the music around Hofhaimer's circle we can get a good impression of what was happening. The earliest pieces are little more than arrangements of vocal works, while the later ones, though often based on chant melodies, display a heavily ornamented idiom far removed from vocal style. The keyboard music of other countries follows the same pattern. In Italy, for instance, the first keyboard publication (1517) was nothing more than arrangements of 26 frottole with elaborate embellishments of the upper parts. As time went on keyboard music became both increasingly improvisatory and increasingly contrapuntal. The greatest composers were the Spaniard Antonio de Cabezón and the Italians Girolamo Cavazzoni (c. 1525–c. 1577), Andrea Gabrieli (c. 1520–86), Claudio Merulo (1533–1604), and Giovanni de Macque (c. 1552–1614). Merulo and de Macque paved the way to the Baroque: Merulo (of whom it is said audiences "crushed one another in their eagerness to hear him") with his concise motives, de Macque with his far-reaching chromatic harmonies—a good example is his *Consonanze stravaganti* (Roving Harmonies). The French tended to be more conservative, writing mainly dances and vocal arrangements. The last important French keyboard composer, Jean Titelouze (1563–1633), specialized in variations on hymns and magnificats possibly intended to serve a liturgical function.

Keyboard Music: England

As good as the above composers were, we must look to England for the greatest flowering of Renaissance keyboard music. Beginning around the middle of the 16th century, British composers began producing vast quantities of keyboard works in virtually all the genres that have been described—dances, preludes, programmatic works, fantasias, transcription of madrigals and other vocal pieces, and, above all, variations. Much of this music was designed for household use, but much of it was also of formidable virtuosity, hardly suitable for the amateur. The principal collections were the Mulliner Book (c. 1540–1585), primarily for organ, the *Parthenia* (1611), and the Fitzwilliam Virginal Book (c. 1620). These two latter anthologies were intended not for organ or harpsichord, but for the harpsichord-like virginal (a word which could also refer generically to any sort of plucked keyboard instrument). Among the major British keyboard composers—all represented in the above compilations—were John Redford, Thomas Tallis, Thomas Tomkins, Peter Philips, Giles Farnaby, John Bull, Orlando Gibbons, and William Byrd. The most impressive collection by a single composer is Byrd's *My Ladye Nevell's Booke* (1591), a compendium of nearly every important keyboard genre of the time.

Dance
Social dancing occupied a higher place during the Renaissance than at any time before or since. No social occasion of any importance was complete without dancing, and some of the dances were of such complexity and difficulty that it is hard to imagine anyone but professionals mastering them. While detailed contemporary information exists on the proper method of executing dances in works such as Thoinot Arbeau's *Orchesography* (1588), few clues survive pertaining to such musical issues as tempo, orchestration, and ornamentation. Specific instrumentation is almost never indicated for ensemble dances, nor are such niceties as dynamics and articulation. Great freedom is therefore granted the 20th-century performer and, for all we know, may have been granted his Renaissance counterparts. But this does not mean anything goes. Music intended for actual dancing, which includes most of the principal collections published by such figures as Attaignant, Susato, Gervaise, Moderne, and Phalese and Praetorius, must be performed at tempos slow enough to allow the dancers to execute their steps. Modern concert realizations, I fear, are almost uniformly too brisk. Such restrictions of course need not apply to the stylized dance music that became increasingly popular toward the end of the Renaissance; this is meant for listening, not dancing. In it the dances are typically grouped into suites, and enriched with fuller, more contrapuntal textures than music for dancing. The occasion must also be considered. Indoor performances naturally demand relatively intimate orchestration; "loud" instruments like shawms would be out of place in this context.

Theatre
Instruments also played a major role at theatrical events. The most notable such were comedies, which traditionally were enhanced by the insertion between acts of musical *intermezzi* or *intermedii*. These entertainments were especially popular at important royal ceremonies such as the wedding of Cosimo de'Medici and Eleonora of Toledo in Florence in 1539 (music by Francesco Corteccia), and subsequent Medici marriages. At such ceremonies the *intermedii*, with their spectacular staging, lavish orchestration, and elaborate dances and costumes, commanded more attention than the play itself. This drove one Florentine playwright, Antonfrancesco Grazzini, to complain in 1565: "Once one went in for *intermedii* in order to fill out a comedy, and now comedy is written for the *intermedii*." Instruments of every sort were used, generally within an established symbolic framework: trumpets for instance were appropriate for accompanying nobility, trombones for infernal scenes, winds for pastoral settings. The instruments were not supplied with idiomatic music of their own (their precise allocation was rarely designated) but served to double or alternate with the voices.

Their role was to point up the action and above all to add color. *Intermedii* provided a starting point for Baroque opera; Monteverdi's opulent orchestration to *Orfeo*, in fact, comes directly from the *intermedii* tradition.

SELECTED RECORDINGS

The foremost development among early music instrumentalists in the past few decades has been the emergence of musicians who not merely perform Renaissance music on Renaissance instruments, but do so using Renaissance techniques. Consider the lute. Julian Bream and Konrad Ragossnig, as fine as they are, essentially approach it as a relative of the modern Spanish guitar; they play a compromise instrument, sturdier in construction and with higher string tension than the Renaissance lute. The result is a bigger, mellower, but less delicate sound than that obtained in the Renaissance. Today, thanks to the efforts of such players as Bream and Ragossnig in popularizing the lute repertoire, we now have a host of brilliant young lutenists who have gone a step further and mastered authentic instruments and playing methods. These include Paul O'Dette, James Tyler, Hopkinson Smith, Anthony Bailes, and Toyohiko Satoh. Similar tales could be told with nearly every other Renaissance instrument, as may readily be heard on the recordings by the instrumentalists of the Early Music Consort of London, Musica Reservata, Consort of Musicke, and the many other first-rate early music ensembles encountered in the pages of this book.

Introduction

*INSTRUMENTS OF THE MIDDLE AGES AND RENAISSANCE
David Munrow and the Early Music Consort of London. Includes 98-page illustrated book by Munrow
Angel SBX-3810 or EMI HMV SLS 988 (two discs)

Accordingly we probably are closer to the true sound of Renaissance instruments today than at any time since the Renaissance. No finer introduction to those sounds could be imagined than David Munrow's book cum recordings *Instruments of the Middle Ages and Renaissance,* a stunning achievement discussed in detail in Chapter 5.

Lute Music

*LUTE MUSIC OF THE RENAISSANCE
Eugen M. Dombois, Renaissance lute
EMI Electrola SME 81033
DOWLAND: THE COMPLETE LUTE MUSIC
Anthony Bailes, Jakob Lindberg, Nigel North, Anthony Rooley, and Christopher Wilson, lutenists
L'Oiseau-Lyre Florilegium D187 D5 (five discs)
BAKFARK: THE COMPLETE LUTE MUSIC
Daniel Benkö, lute
Available individually as Hungaroton SLPX 11549; 11817; 11893; 11987/88
LUTE MUSIC OF THE RENAISSANCE
Konrad Ragossnig, lute
France (DG Archiv 2533 304); Spain (2533 183); England (2533 157); Italy (2533 173); Eastern Europe (2533 294); Germany and the Netherlands (2533 302)

SPANISH VIHUELA MUSIC. DAZA/NARVÁEZ/PISADOR
Musical Heritage Society/MHS 3331
MILAN/VALDERRÁBANO
(MHS 1894)
FUENLLANA/MUDARRA
Jorge Fresno, vihuela
MHS 3077
*THE ENGLISH LUTE: DOWLAND AND BYRD
Paul O'Dette, lutes
Nonesuch H-71363
ITALIAN LUTE DUETS FROM THE 16TH AND EARLY 17TH
CENTURIES
Hopkinson Smith and Paul O'Dette, assorted lutes
Seraphim S-60631
*MUSIC OF THE RENAISSANCE VIRTUOSI
James Tyler, lute, baroque guitar, mandora. With Nigel North, lute,
theorbo, cittern; Douglas Wootton, lute, bandora; Jane Ryan, bass
viol
Nonesuch H-71389 or Saga 5438

Collectors of instrumental music have an almost unlimited wealth of excellent recorded material to explore. The lute and vihuela repertoire, for instance, has been outstandingly well served on record. To my mind the ideal starting point is Dombois' well-chosen selection of English, French, German, and Spanish pieces. Dombois was one of the earliest modern lutenists to master authentic Renaissance techniques and instruments; alas, his career was cut short in its prime by arthritis. The magnitude of our loss is evident on his Electrola album: Dombois manages to find the appropriate style for each piece, and does so with a directness of approach, beauty of sound, and unpresuming technical wizardry that compels the highest admiration.

Among the noteworthy multi-record projects to appear in the last decade are Ragossnig's six-disc survey of the major lute repertoire, the Argentinian Jorge Fresno's three-disc overview of the seven major vihuela collections, Daniel Benko's comprehensive Bakfark series, and the complete Dowland lute music. If Ragossnig at times makes his instrument sound more like a guitar than a lute, this is to take nothing away from his considerable musical and technical attainments. Julian Bream may be grouped in the same class as Ragossnig, but he is an even better musician: his playing is so colorful, expressively molded, and breathtakingly virile that the manner in which he achieves his results becomes a moot question. The same might be said of Andrés Segovia, who unapologetically plays the lute repertoire on the guitar. There is no need to list their many recordings; nearly any of them will provide ample pleasure.

Fresno is not such a refined technician as these artists, but his playing of the difficult vihuela (which has a crisper sound, with less carrying power than the lute) is deeply felt and stylistically keen. As usual with Hispavox's History of Spanish Music series, extensive and highly informative annotations accompany the albums. Though Benkö may not be the most subtle or inspired of lutenists, his loving attention to Bakfark extensively enriches our knowledge of one of the foremost lutenist-composers of the entire Renaissance. A similar service is being systematically provided for other major lute composers by an astonishingly gifted generation of young lutenists. An ideal place to sample the abilities of this new generation of lutenists is through the magnificent complete Dowland album cited above, which L'Oiseau-Lyre cleverly allots to five different players. As a single-disc introduction to the English lute, Paul O'Dette's bargain-priced Nonesuch offering is highly recommended.

Solo Viol Music

*ORTIZ: "RICERCADAS" FROM THE TRATADO DE GLOSAS (1553)
Jordi Savall, viola da gamba. With Genoveva Galvez, harpsichord and positive organ; and Sergi Cassademunt, tenor viola da gamba
Musical Heritage Society MHS 1888
LESSONS FOR THE LYRA-VIOLL
Music by Corkine, Ferrabosco I, and Anon. Jordi Savall, lyra-viol and bass viol
Astrée AS 51

Multi-Disc Keyboard Anthologies

MASTERS OF EARLY ENGLISH KEYBOARD MUSIC
Thuston Dart, harpsichord, clavichord, and organ
L'Oiseau-Lyre OLS 114-8 (five discs, available separately)
*BYRD: MY LADYE NEVELL'S BOOKE (1591)
Christopher Hogwood, virginal, organ, and harpsichords
L'Oiseau-Lyre Florilegium D29D 4 (four discs). Excerpts available on DSLO 566

Keyboard: Harpsichord, Virginal, Clavichord, Spinet

GIBBONS: KEYBOARD MUSIC
Christopher Hogwood, harpsichord and organ
L'Oiseau-Lyre Florilegium DSLO 515
*THE GOLDEN AGE OF HARPSICHORD MUSIC
Rafael Puyana, harpsichord
Mercury SR 90304
16TH-CENTURY ENGLISH KEYBOARD MUSIC
Trevor Pinnock, harpsichord
Vanguard 71262 or CRD 1050
THE ENGLISH VIRGINALISTS
Gustav Leonhardt, harpsichord
Harmonia Mundi 20 308

Those other chief solo instrumental categories of the Renaissance—the viola da gamba and various keyboard instruments—have also been graced in recent years by a young crop of players of thoroughgoing mastery: I think in particular of the gambist Jordi Savall and keyboardists Christopher Hogwood, Colin Tilney, and Trevor Pinnock. Any of their recordings come highly recommended.

But my first choice for an introduction to the harpsichord music of the Renaissance would be a 20-year-old album played on a decidedly inauthentic Pleyel by the now middle-aged Columbian Rafael Puyana. Puyana's technique is so dazzling, his disposition so fiery that one listens mesmerized to his virtuosity. This record has inexcusably been unavailable for a number of years;

no collector should pass up the opportunity to acquire it. The most impressive Renaissance selections on Puyana's disc are English—hardly surprising, since the English did more for the harpsichord than any other country.

Taken *in toto,* my recommended recordings of English keyboard music cover pretty much the entire range of the British Renaissance accomplishment. Many feature mean-tone (unequal) temperament and period instruments. The most comprehensive large-scale survey of this repertoire is Thurston Dart's *Masters of Early English Keyboard Music,* five discs recorded between 1955–63. Featured are numerous works by such central composers as Byrd, Tomkins, Bull, Gibbons, and Farnaby, and there is an extensive selection by a host of other figures. Nor are the choices limited to the harpsichord literature—a fair number of organ and clavichord works are also included. Dart was one of the leaders of the British early music revival that has reached such a lofty level today. He set a very high standard. He plays all his instruments with a winning blend of elegance, verve, and scholarship, exhibiting a remarkable comprehension of many different styles. Though Dart incorporates early fingering techniques, he does not use period instruments. Christopher Hogwood does, however, on his complete recording of Byrd's *My Ladye Nevell's Booke,* the foremost collection of keyboard music by a single composer in the entire Renaissance. Hogwood employs four different instruments: a 1611 Ruckers virginal; a chamber organ modelled on English instruments of Byrd's time, an Italian harpsichord based on late 16th-century specimens, and a Flemish harpsichord built on the model of a 1638 Rucker. All sound distinctive and eminently appropriate for the music they here serve. A variety of tunings are used, both mean-tone and equal. This is a landmark album.

Keyboard: Organ

*SOUNDS OF 16TH-CENTURY SPAIN
Paul Bernard at the organs of San Jaime, Calatayud and Santa Maria, Darocca
Angel S-36914. 24 selections, by Joan de Segovia, Palero, Pedro de Soto, Bruna, Diego de Torrijos, and Moreno

CABEZÓN: ORGAN MUSIC
P. Paulino Ortiz, organs of Covarrubias and Daroca
Musical Heritage Society OR 436

HISPANIAE MUSICAE: ORGAN WORKS OF THE 16TH CENTURY
Julio-M. García Llovera and Montserrat Torrent Serra at organs in Barcelona, Toledo, and Zaragoza
DG Archiv 198 455. 16 selections by 10 composers

A SURVEY OF THE WORLD'S GREATEST ORGAN MUSIC: FRANCE, VOLUME I
Andre Isoir and Xavier Darasse, organists
Vox SVBX-5310 (three discs). Includes music by Courroy, Costeley, Jannequin, Sermisy, Attaignant, Le Jeune, Titelouze. Titelouze/Attaignant album available separately as Turnabout TV 34126S

*HISTORIC ORGANS OF EUROPE: FREDERIKSBORG, COMPENIUS ORGAN (1612)
Francis Chapelet, organ
Oryx 1752 or CBS Odyssey 32-16-0068

BULL: SELECTED WORKS
Francis Cameron, organ; Susi Jeans, virginal; Gamben-Consort
Johannes Koch
DG Archiv 198 472

The principal Renaissance keyboard instrument on the Continent
was the organ. Unfortunately not much of this repertoire has
been decently recorded; I list the best of a limited group. That
one exception—and it is a major one—is Spanish organ music. To
properly appreciate this music, it must be heard on a Spanish
Renaissance organ. Such organs, with their silvery overcast and
raspy, intensely penetrating *trompeta* stops, could not be confused with the instruments of any other country. No words can
begin to do justice to their thrilling sound. There have been quite
a few memorable recordings of these organs, several of which I
have listed; together they provide an excellent overview of the
Spanish achievement. Start with Paul Bernard's rousing
collection—a true spirit-lifter—then move on to the MHS Cabezón disc.

Dance Music

DANCES OF THE COURTS AND VILLAGES FROM THE SIXTEENTH CENTURY
La Grande Ecurie et la Chambre du Roy; Florilegium Musicum de
Paris; Jean-Claude Malgoire, director
CBS Odyssey Y-34617
*PRAETORIUS: SELECTIONS FROM "TERPSICHORE"; SCHEIN: SUITES FROM "BANCHETTO MUSICALE"; WIDMANN: DANCES
Collegium Terpsichore directed by Fritz Neumeyer
DG Archiv 198 166
*16TH-CENTURY FRENCH DANCE MUSIC
Philips 6500 293
16TH-CENTURY ITALIAN DANCE MUSIC
Philips 6500 102
Musica Reservata conducted by John Beckett
RENAISSANCE DANCE MUSIC from collections by Moderne,
Ferdinand Conrad and ensemble
Quintessence PMC 7088
Clemencic Consort of Vienna; René Clemencic, director
Musical Heritage Society MHS 3938. Identical selections on both discs

---

Renaissance dance music is so intrinsically delightful and so filled
with opportunities for the creative performer that it has inevitably received an abundance of recordings. Many of them go more
than a bit overboard, but most are pleasantly entertaining. There
is surely no need for me to provide a comprehensive listing here.
My long-time personal favorites are: for the 16th-century repertoire, Malgoire's Odyssey disc; for the early 17th-century repertoire, the venerable Archive album. Both are uncommonly imaginative and exhilarating, even if the orchestrations are probably
more fantastical than authentic. I list the Conrad and Clemencic
discs not because they are superior to their competitors (though
they are certainly good), but because both offer the *identical*
selection of pieces and so provide an ideal opportunity to compare the strikingly different realizations possible with any given

dance. The Musica Reservata's anthologies, performed with their usual enthusiasm and cutting edge, are particularly valuable since the group prefaces many of the instrumental dances with the songs on which they were based. Numerous fine dance selections may in fact be found embedded within essentially vocal collections; the Musica Reservata and Early Music Consort of London are especially fond of this practice.

Anthologies of (Mostly) Ayres, Part Songs, and Consort Music

MUSIC OF SHAKESPEARE'S TIME: VOCAL AND INSTRUMENTAL WORKS OF ELIZABETHAN ENGLAND
Assorted soloists and groups
Nonesuch HB-73010
*WILLIAM BYRD AND HIS CONTEMPORARIES
The London Early Music Consort directed by James Typer
RCA RL 25110/(2); or RCA CRL 2-2794 (two discs)

Consort Songs and Consort Music

WILLIAM BYRD AND HIS AGE: DIVERS SONGS FOR VOICE AND VIOLS
Alfred Deller, countertenor; Wenzinger Consort of Viols of the Schola Cantorum Basiliensis, August Wenzinger, director
Vanguard Bach Guild BG-557
DOWLAND: LACHRIMAE, OR SEVEN TEARES (1604)
Consort of Musicke directed by Anthony Rooley
L'Oiseau-Lyre Florilegium DSLO517
GIBBONS: FANTAISIES ROYALES
Jordi Savall, Christophe Coin, Sergi Casademunt, viols; Johannes Sonnleitner, positif
Astrée AS 43
WILLIAM LAWES: CONSORT MUSIC
Consort of Musicke, Anthony Rooley, director
L'Oiseau-Lyre Florilegium DSLO 560, 564, 573, 574
Elizabethan Consort directed by Thurston Dart
Argo ZRG 555
DOWLAND: CONSORT MUSIC
Extempore String Ensemble
Hypèrion A66010
*MORLEY: DANCES FOR BROKEN CONSORT FROM THE "FIRST BOOKE OF CONSORT LESSONS" (1599)
The Early Music Consort of London and The Morley Consort directed by David Munrow
Angel S-36851 or EMI HQS 1249
*FLORID SONG AND GAMBA MUSIC IN ENGLAND c. 1610–1660
Studio der Frühen Musik; Concertus Musicus of Vienna
Telefunken Das Alte Werk SAWT 9472
*ENGLISH MUSIC FOR RECORDERS AND CONSORT OF VIOLA
Brüggen Consort led by Frans Brüggen
Telefunken Das Alte Werk SAWT 9511
MUSICK FOR VOYCES & VIOLLS
The New England Consort of Viols; Grace Feldman, director. With Jane Bryden, soprano; Jeffrey Gall, countertenor; Frank Hoffmeister, tenor
Titanic Ti-26

The bulk of the Renaissance consort literature—with or without voices—is English. And the English have recorded this wonderful music in such profusion and with such distinction that one can practically pick and choose. Perhaps the best place to start is through two fine anthologies, Nonesuch's *Music of Shakespeare's Time* and RCA's *William Byrd and His Contemporaries*. The former concentrates on the late 16th century, the latter on the early 17th century. When taken together, a comprehensive picture of the secular music of the English Renaissance emerges. And the performances, particularly those of Tyler's RCA group, maintain an admirably high standard. The RCA album also includes thrilling one-to-a-part renditions of three Byrd motets.

But the British are not the only ones to do justice to their music. Ample proof comes from the Brüggen Consort's heavenly recorder/viol disc, the Gibbons album by Savall and company, and the combined efforts of the Vienna Concertus Musicus and Studio der Frühen Musik (as well as assisting British artists) in an inspired program of virtuoso song and gamba music. Americans can also do the English consort repertoire well, as the Titanic disc splendidly reveals.

Solo Songs, Ayres, and Part Songs

*O Mistress Mine: Elizabethan Lute Songs and Italian Songs
James Bowman, countertenor; Robert Spencer, lute and chitarrone. With Dennis Nesbitt, treble viol; and Oliver Brookes, bass viol
Seraphim S-60323 or EMI HQS 1281

Elizabethan Lute Songs and Solos
Frank Patterson, tenor; Robert Spencer, lute
Philips 6500 282

Elizabethan Lute Songs
RCA LSC-3131

Dowland: 6 Lute Songs
RCA LSC-2819
Peter Pears, tenor; Julian Bream, lute

*English Ayres and Duets Sung in Authentic Elizabethan Pronunciation
The Camerata of London: Glenda Simpson, mezzo-soprano; Paul Hillier, baritone; Barry Mason, lute; Rosemary Thorndycraft, bass viol
Hypèrion A6603

Dowland: The Complete Music
Series in progress. Assorted volumes, most performed by The Consort of Musicke, Anthony Rooley, director
L'Oiseau-Lyre Florilegium

*Canciones Espanolas: Songs from the Middle Ages and Renaissance
Teresa Berganza, mezzo-soprano; Narciso Yepes, guitar
DG 2530 504 (see Chapter 9)

Morley: The First Booke of Ayres
Nigel Rogers, tenor; Nikolaus Harnoncourt, viola da gamba; Eugen Dombois, lute
Telefunken Das Alte Werk 6.41127

I am not consistently happy with the recorded performances of solo lute songs. Most strike me as unduly precious. Accordingly,

I have a fondness for the refreshingly direct approach of the Irish tenor Frank Patterson. But the most stimulating disc of ayres is that by the Camerata of London, sung with considerable affect but without mannerism in "authentic Elizabethan pronunciation." The effect can be startling. And no lute song connoisseur should overlook the long-esteemed achievements of Deller, Dupré, Pears, and Bream, or of the younger generation of British singers represented on such labels as Argo and L'Oiseau-Lyre (whose Dowland series is a tremendous contribution). For the Spanish vihuela song repertoire Berganza/Yepes provide an exceptionally persuasive introduction.

Courtly Entertainment Music

*MUSIC OF THE WAITS
Ensemble directed by Don Smithers
Argo ZRG 646
*A FLORENTINE FESTIVAL: MUSIC FOR FERDINAND DE MEDICI
Musica Reservata conducted by John Beckett
Argo ZRG 602
LA PELLEGRINA 1589: Intermedii and Concerti for the Wedding of Grand Duke Ferdinand I de'Medici to Christina of Lorraine
Stockholm Chamber Choir and soloists, Eric Ericson, artistic director. Linde-Consort; Hans-Martin Linde, director
EMI Electrola Reflexe 1C 165-30114/15 (two discs)

There are few opportunities to hear the sort of town music provided by the German *Stadtpfeifer*, Italian *piffari*, and English *waits*, for the simple reason that most of their repertoire was memorized and orally transmitted and consequently does not survive. But Don Smithers has compiled an enchanting collection of the types of pieces heard at formal British entertainments on his *Music of the Waits* album. I have long cherished this record, and with good cause: the music is delectable, the orchestration marvellously colorful, and the playing electrifyingly good (among the musicians are David Munrow and James Tyler).

The most resplendent Renaissance entertainment music was that composed for the Florentine *intermedii*. One of the most sumptuous of these occasions was the 1589 Medici wedding. All six of its *intermedii* are presented on Electrola's *La Pellegrina* album, while the second and sixth are featured on the Musica Reservata's *A Florentine Festival*. Musica Reservata's performances are sprightlier and more virtuosic; the Electrola forces are sometimes on the heavy side, but they nonetheless amply convey the magnificence of the event. And how extravagant some of this music is: Cristofano Malvezzi's *O fortunato giorno*, heard on both discs, calls for a 30 vocal parts divided into seven choirs. The value of the Argo album is enhanced by a lovely selection of frottole, madrigals, dances, and dance songs.

Ornamentation

THE ART OF ORNAMENTATION AND EMBELLISHMENT IN THE RENAISSANCE AND BAROQUE
Various soloists and groups
Vanguard Bach Guild HM 47/8 (two discs)

VIRTUOSO ORNAMENTATION AROUND 1600
Schola Cantorum Basiliensis
Harmonia Mundi Germany 1C 165-99895 6 (two discs)

While improvised embellishment has become accepted as an integral part of Baroque music-making, performers of Renaissance music have for the most part adopted a surprisingly conservative attitude towards this practice. And yet we know that embellishment was expected in virtually every kind of Renaissance piece, sacred polyphony not excepted. Indeed, there is a substantial didactic literature illustrating just how to go about ornamenting chansons, madrigals, and motets. Precisely such didactic examples are featured on the Vanguard and Harmonia Mundi ornamentation albums; the Vanguard is particularly instructive, for it supplies the unadorned pieces alongside the embellished versions. Yet the contents of these discs are deceiving. For one thing, the examples almost certainly illustrate not actual practice, but rather the range of possibilites. The real thing would have been less extravagant and artificial. Moreover, it would have been extemporized. Essentially all these modern-day performers do is play the written-out embellishments; a sense of spontaneity has been lost. And spontaneity is the whole point of any ornamental practice. In general, probably the finest examples of improvised embellishment in serious music are the releases of Binkley and his group (lighter repertoire, such as dance music, tends to bring out more of the ham in performers). A striking recent application of extensive embellishment to the consort literature is the appropriately named Extempore String Ensemble's Dowland album (Hypèrion A66010). There exists a pressing need for more enlightened experimentaton of this sort, in the sacred polyphonic repertoire above all—whether or not you immediately like the result. For only through doing can we achieve mastery.

11

THE LATE RENAISSANCE

The Madrigal

By the middle of the 16th century the focus of progressive musical thought had shifted to the country already responsible for the creative impetus in the other arts—Italy. The madrigal had become the principal secular genre, and, as in the case of the ballade in the late Middle Ages, was now a vehicle for virtuoso composition and performance. No composer worth his salt neglected the madrigal. The Netherlanders Orlando di Lasso (1532-94) and Philippe de Monte (1521-1603) expanded upon the techniques of Rore; Monte published the incredible total of 1,100 madrigals in 41 volumes.

But it was in the hands of the Netherlander Giaches de Wert (1535-96) and three Italians, Luca Marenzio (1553-1599), Carlo Gesualdo (c. 1560-1613), and Claudio Monteverdi (1567-1643) that the expressive potential of the madrigal was extended to its furthest reaches. Texts were selected with their musical possibilities in mind. Every phrase, even every word received its own unique musical characterization; the intent was to graphically convey all the moods and meanings of the poetry. In so doing the smooth imitative polyphony of the international style was replaced by music of an impulsive character full of abrupt shifts of tempo and texture. As a result, each piece possessed a highly individual character. The madrigal's chief musical problem was organization: success or failure depended almost entirely on the composer's ability to maintain attention through the vividness of his response to the text.

In the music of Gesualdo and Monteverdi, these techniques reached the breaking point. Gesualdo's madrigals mirrored his own emotional instability (upon discovering his wife's adultery he murdered her, her lover, and an infant whose parentage he suspected). In search of heightened expressivity, Gesualdo almost willfully fragmented textures, juxtaposed styles, and introduced startling chromaticisms. His music at times conveys a near-overpowering intensity. Monteverdi kept his volatility under better control; indeed, one of his greatest contributions was the manner in which he managed to maintain structural integrity while making "the words the mistress of the harmony." The emancipation of melody, harmony, counterpoint, and texture by Gesualdo and Monteverdi, and also by German Heinrich Schütz (1585–1672), whose Opus 1 (1611) has been judged by some as the finest book of Italian madrigals ever written, left little room for further development. Attempts by Orazio Vecchi (1550–1605), Adriano Banchieri (1567–1634), and others to adapt groups of madrigals to dramatic purposes (the so-called madrigal comedies) were short-lived. The madrigal's dramatic potential awaited fruition in the new, more flexible style of the Baroque. Monteverdi and Schütz in fact went on to become the major figures of the early Baroque. For a brilliant exposition of the differences between Renaissance and Baroque style, see the first chapter of Manfred Bukofzer's *Music in the Baroque Era* (Norton, 1947).

But the story of the madrigal did not end here. As with so much else in the Renaissance, the final tale was to be told in England. The British appropriated the Italian manner for their own purposes and in their own language. The first completely English madrigal publication was Thomas Morley's *First Book of Madrigals for Four Voices* (1594). Morley also edited and published a collection of 25 madrigals by as many composers entitled *The Triumphes of Oriana* (1601). Among the most important British madrigalists were Morley, Giles Farnaby, Francis Pilkington, John Bennet, John Wilbye, John Ward, Thomas Weelkes, and Thomas Tomkins. The English madrigals, especially the earlier ones, tended to be lighter in spirit and subject matter than the Italian model; Morley even adopted the fa-la-la balletto style of Gastoldi. Nonetheless, they reveal a remarkable mastery of declamation and mood. And some of them—particularly pieces by Wilbye, Weelkes, and Gibbons—are every bit as moving as their Italian models, without the overwrought Italianate affect.

Protestant Hymns and Polyphony

Developments in late Renaissance sacred music were naturally conditioned by the religious revolutions of the 16th century. Though Martin Luther liberated his church from Rome, he retained much of the Catholic liturgy and music. Luther was himself an amateur composer, singer, lute and flute player, and passionate lover of music. He wrote: "Next to the word of God, only music deserves to be extolled as the mistress and governess of human feelings." Music in the Catholic church had long been the province of Church musicians, whether a chant choir or polyphonic soloists. Without wishing to eliminate either, Luther at the same time wanted his congregation to participate directly in the musical service. To this end, he contributed the strophic songs known as chorales—the equivalent of what we today call hymns. These chorales were monophonic pieces in the vernacular, often with quite complicated rhythms (alas, these marvelous rhythmic complexities have been evened out in modern transcriptions). Luther was not above taking a popular secular tune ("The devil does not need all the good tunes for himself") and replacing or altering the words so as to achieve a properly reverent text. Such pieces were called *contrafacta*. One of the most famous was Isaac's touching lied *Innsbruck, ich muss dich lassen*.

Before long Protestant composers began using these chorale tunes as the subject matter for polyphonic compositions. They were set in a variety of ways: in straightforward chordal style with the melody in the soprano; in cantus firmus fashion with the chorale in long notes in the tenor and free counterpoint in the remaining voices; or in classic Franco-Flemish imitative style, with each phrase of the chorale supplying the imitative subject. These settings were intended for performance by the choir; a common method of realization was to alternate verses of the monophonic chorale sung by the congregation with the choir's singing of the polyphonic version, perhaps with instrumental assistance. Among the major composers of polyphonic chorale settings were Johann Walther (1496–1570), Thomas Stoltzer, and Ludwig Senfl.

Their settings, however complex, always kept the chorale tune and text intact. Toward the end of the century, however, German Protestant composers began employing chorale melodies with considerable freedom, using them as the starting point for large-scale polyphonic pieces. Among the foremost composers of such chorale motets were Hans Leo Hassler (1564–1612), equally well-known for his Italianate secular works, Michael Praetorius (1571–1621), and Johann Hermann Schein (1586–1630)—the latter two carried the Renaissance tradition over into the Baroque.

France was not so lucky. Jean Calvin (1509–64) and other French Protestants, though not necessarily music haters, were suspicious of its place in public worship. The principal French contribution to the musical liturgy was the French Psalter of 1562, settings of psalm texts translated into French with melodies written or selected by Loys Bourgeois (c. 1510–c. 1561). Like the German chorales, these were monophonic pieces intended for unaccompanied congregational singing. Because of the Calvinist prohibitions against complicated music in the church, however, these tunes were rarely utilized as material for large-scale vocal and instrumental music. Nonetheless, fairly simple motet-like settings were cultivated by such figures as Claude Goudimel (c. 1505–72), Claude le Jeune (c. 1525/1600), and the Dutch composer Jan Sweelinck (c. 1562–1621). These were intended not for the church but for private devotional use at home.

Catholic Music of the Counter-Reformation

Meanwhile, the Catholic Church was experiencing troubled times. The Protestant Reformation in the North and the threatened loss of England and much of Eastern Europe to Protestantism pressed home the need for internal reforms. These reforms were conveyed in the decrees of the Council of Trent (1545–63), which sought both to correct abuses in the Church administration and to uphold the validity of traditional doctrine against the sweeping changes of the Reformers. With respect to music the

Catholic desires were predictable: emotional excess and virtuoso artifice were to be avoided, and the words of the liturgy should always be clear. Moreover, Church music should remain in Latin.

Giovanni Pierluigi de Palestrina (c. 1525–94), the chief musical figure of the Counter-Reformation, revered for the refinement and perfection of his sacred counterpoint.

The major musical figure of the Counter Reformation was Giovanni Pierluigi de Palestrina (c. 1525–94). More than any other composer, Palestrina came to represent the ideal of the Renaissance. His sober, diatonic idiom was isolated and imitated throughout the succeeding centuries as the model of pure counterpoint. Even today his style serves as the basis of modal counterpoint training for music theory students. There can be no doubt about Palestrina's greatness. If his music lacks the emotional fervor of Josquin, Lasso, or Victoria, it nonetheless embodies to the last degree a perfection of detail, an uncanny command of sonority, a wistful resignation and a rarefied spirituality. And his expressive range is by no means narrow.

No contemporary Italian church composer could match him. The best of his Catholic colleagues were his pupil Giovanni Maria Nanino (c. 1545–1607), who later became director of the Papal Chapel, and Felice Anerio (1560–1614), a pupil of Nanino who at Palestrina's death succeeded him as official composer to the Papal Chapel. But the greatest heir to Palestrina's style was the Spaniard, Tomás Luis de Victoria (c. 1549–1611), who probably studied with the master while in Rome from c. 1565–80. Victoria was a musician of unusual devoutness. In 1575 he was ordained as a priest, and spent most of his career at one religious institution or another; his final decades, from 1586–1611, were spent in a Madrid convent in service of the Empress Maria. Victoria's style miraculously merges Palestrina's mastery of counterpoint and declamation with the mystical intensity of such significant Spanish predecessors as Juan Vásquez (c. 1500–

c. 1560), Juan Navarro (c. 1525–1580), Christóbal de Morales (c. 1500–1553), and Morales' pupil, Francesco Guerrero (1527/8–1599). Victoria is a far more dramatic composer than Palestrina, unafraid to employ striking dissonances or melodic leaps to intensify an important textual point. Donald Grout aptly compared Palestrina's art to that of Raphael, Victoria's to that of El Greco.

Venice

Rome was not the only city in Italy to exert far-reaching influence in sacred music. The most progressive sacred music was in fact being written in and around St. Mark's Cathedral in Venice, which under the directorship of Adrian Willaert (c. 1490–1562) had become the center for polychoral music. Willaert's pupil Andrea Gabrieli (c. 1520–86) and Andrea's nephew Giovanni (1557–1612) expanded Willaert's experiments, writing numerous antiphonal works for three or more choirs of both voices and concerted instruments. Giovanni's music especially—with its emphasis on contrasting motives, exploitation of tone color and acoustics, rhythmic virility, and short recurring sections in lieu of traditional flowing imitative counterpoint—must properly be classified as belonging to the Baroque era.

Lasso

The culmination of the Franco-Flemish style comes in the works of Giaches de Wert and Philippe de Monte, whose greatest contributions were probably their madrigals, and above all in the figure of Orlando di Lasso (1532–94). Lasso was born in Mons, trained in Italy, and from 1556 until his death worked for Albert V, Duke of Bavaria, eventually becoming the official court composer. He was probably the most widely travelled and versatile of all Renaissance composers. His formidable musical talents were quickly spotted: Lasso's singing voice was reputedly so

Orlando di Lasso (1532–94), most cosmopolitan of Renaissance composers, master of all the important styles sacred and secular... in the French, German, Italian, and Latin languages.

beautiful that he was kidnapped three times while still a boy. Lasso was incredibly prolific; his 2000-plus compositions reveal a mind-boggling mastery of Latin church music, the German lied, Italian madrigal, French chanson, and much more. He was knighted by both Emperor Maximilian II and the Pope. As might be expected from such a worldly man, the heart of Lasso's output—his more than 500 motets—reveals a strong personality of great humanity, with a richer coloristic and harmonic palette and a far more passionate temperament than his almost exact contemporary Palestrina. Lasso was especially revered for his genius at bringing out every nuance of mood in his texts.

English Sacred Music

But the true zenith of Renaissance church music occurred not on the Continent but in England. England, as has been noted, underwent its own religious revolution, having officially converted to Protestantism during the reign of Henry VIII (with a five-year return to Catholicism under the short-lived rule of Mary Tudor). Yet, paradoxically, the greatest composer of English sacred music, William Byrd, was a Catholic. Despite the handicap of his religion, Byrd managed to thrive in his career. From 1570 until his death some 50 years later he served as an organist at the Chapel Royal. His music was so admired that together with Thomas Tallis, then the grand old man of English musical life, Byrd was given a monopoly on the printing of music in England. As their first venture Tallis and Byrd collaborated on a collection of 34 motets, 17 apiece, under the title *Cantiones Sacrae (1575)*; Byrd contributed two further volumes in 1589 and 1591. Though these collections include relatively few liturgical works, Byrd in his *Gradualia* of 1605 and 1607 created the most important collection of Mass and Office Propers since Isaac's *Choralis Constantinus*. Byrd also wrote three Latin Masses. These Catholic liturgical pieces were composed and published under great risk, and with no apparent prospects of performance, for public observance of the Catholic Mass was forbidden under the reigns of both Elizabeth and James; one person was even arrested for possessing Byrd's 1605 *Gradualia*. We can be grateful for Byrd's persistence, for his Catholic works contain music of surpassing beauty. So does his Anglican sacred output, seemingly no less heartfelt despite Byrd's religious leanings. These took the form of *Services*, the Anglican counterpart to the Catholic Mass, and *anthems*, the English analogue of the Latin motet. Anthems were of two sorts: *full*, for unaccompanied chorus; and *verse*, which alternated soloists and chorus and generally had an instrumental accompaniment of organ and/or viols.

Byrd incorporates continental imitative practice naturally and inevitably into remarkably eventful counterpoint which, despite its frequent density of texture and lack of extroverted pictorialism, manages to quietly convey the sense of the text. The sonorities are wonderfully ethereal, yet never static, precisely the sort of music you would imagine hearing upon entering Heaven. The same might be said of Byrd's three successors as writers of Anglican anthems, Protestants all: Thomas Weelkes (c. 1575–1623), the very long-lived Thomas Tomkins (1572–1656), and Orlando Gibbons (1583–1625). In such pieces as

Tomkins' full anthem *When David Heard* and Gibbons's verse anthem *This is the Record of John,* technical considerations hardly seem relevant. The inspiration appears to emanate from some direct line with the Creator, imparting deep profundities with the lightest of brushstrokes. No greater music was written in any era.

SELECTED RECORDINGS

The Virtuoso Italian Madrigal

ITALIAN MADRIGALS
The Abbey Singers
American Decca DL 710103. Eight madrigals by Arcadelt, Rore, Willaert, Verdelot, Wert, Luzzaschi, and A. Gabrieli

AMOROUS DIALOGUS OF THE RENAISSANCE
Accademia Monteverdiana; Denis Stevens, director
Nonesuch H-71232. Ten pieces by Wert, Demantius, Lasso, A. and G. Gabrieli, Hassler, Demantius, Morley, and Willaert

GESUALDO: 7 MADRIGALS FROM BOOK V; MOTETS AND RESPONSORIES
Accademia Monteverdiana; Denis Stevens, conductor
Pye Virtuoso TPLS 13012

*MARENZIO: 10 MADRIGALS FOR 5 AND 6 VOICES
Concerto Vocale, with Konrad Junghänel, lute and theorbo
Harmonia Mundi HM 1065

MONTEVERDI: MADRIGALS, BOOKS III AND IV (complete)
Ensemble and Glyndebourne Opera Chorus directed by Raymond Leppard
Philips 6703 035 (three discs). Book III available separately as Philips 9502 008

VECCHI: "L'AMFIPARNASO," A MADRIGAL COMEDY
The Western Wind
Nonesuch H-71286

WERT: MUSIC FROM THE COURT OF MANTUA
The Jaye Consort of Viols; Accademia Monteverdian Consort; and Ambrosian Singers under the direction of Denis Stevens
Vanguard Cardinal VCS 10083

Many recordings have been made of the late Italian madrigal repertoire, but not many good ones. This music is horrendously difficult to sing: the ranges are wide, the intervals tricky, the problems of balance exasperating. And it is equally difficult to interpret: the word-painting must vividly be brought out, yet without sacrificing a sense of the large-scale structure.

There are, fortunately, some more-than-acceptable recordings; I have listed those that strike me as the most satisfactory. Denis Stevens's work should be singled out. He has surely done more than anyone else in expanding the Italian madrigal discography. But the most memorable album devoted to a single composer is, it seems to me, the Concerto Vocale's recent collection of 10 madrigals by Marenzio, thought by many to be the greatest of all madrigalists. This six-member ensemble utilizes what had probably become the standard disposition for this repertoire by the late 16th century: all men save for a female soprano on the uppermost line. Their performances meet the above requirements: they are sung by a sextet of virtuosos, able to blend seamlessly or emerge individually as the music requires, and able too to illuminate Marenzio's niceties of text setting without destroying appreciation for the whole. The unusual (and very feasible) addition of a lute or theorbo continuo adds to the interest. If you can find it, the Abbey Singers's disc is well worth acquisition. The brilliant singing, featuring the young Jan de Gaetani, is fully up to the demands of the music, as you would expect.

The English Madrigal

*THE TRIUMPHS OF ORIANA
Pro Cantione Antiqua directed by Ian Partridge
DG Archiv 2533 237

*ENGLISH MADRIGALS: 35 MADRIGALS FROM THE OXFORD BOOK OF ENGLISH MADRIGALS
Pro Cantione Antiqua directed by Philip Ledger
Peters International PLE 133/4 (2 discs)

THE KING'S SINGERS SING OF COURTLY PLEASURES: ENGLISH MADRIGALS AND FRENCH CHANSONS
The King's Singers
Angel S-37025. English selection also available paired with Italian madrigals as Moss Music Group MMG 1105 or EMI CSD 3756

*GIBBONS: MADRIGALS AND MOTETS
The Consort of Musicke; Anthony Rooley, director
L'Oiseau-Lyre Florilegium DSLO 512

WEELKES: 19 MADRIGALS
London Stereo Treasury STS 15165

WILBYE: 12 MADRIGALS
STS 15165
London Stereo Treasury
Both recordings by The Wilbye Consort directed by Peter Pears

---

No want of decent representatives afflicts the English madrigal discography. The beginning collector is in fact apt to be overwhelmed by the sheer quantity of desirable choices. Two albums strike me as indispensable, both from the Pro Cantione Antiqua. The first gives complete *The Triumphs of Oriana* (1601), that first great English madrigal collection. With 25 pieces by as many composers, it offers the best single introduction to the early English madrigal. The PCA's second anthology, 35 madrigals by 18 composers, provides the same function for the later repertoire. Their selection is wonderfully unhackneyed, nicely balancing seldom-heard works with such familiar favorites as Morley's *My Bonny Lass She Smileth* and *Now Is the Month of Maying*, Weelkes's *Hark All Ye Lovely Saints*, and Gibbons's almost unbearably poignant *The Silver Swan*. All 35 pieces are conveniently available in the *Oxford Book of English Madrigals*, which should please inveterate score-readers. And the performances (the standard group has been expanded to include female sopranos) are as magnificent as might be expected—full of amazing detail and subtlety.

Equally accomplished are the various English madrigal albums by the King's Singers (see also Chapter 9), the Consort of Musicke, and The Wilbye Consort. I'd unwillingly forego any of them. Their distinctive approaches make for enlightening comparisons.

German Protestant Music

STOLTZER: FOUR GERMAN PSALMS; MISSA "DUPLEX PER TOTUM ANNUM"; MOTETS AND SECULAR MUSIC
Capella Antiqua of Munich conducted by Konrad Ruhland
ABC Seon ABCL-67003/2 (two discs)
SACRED LIEDER AND INSTRUMENTAL WORKS OF LUTHER'S TIME
Studio der Frühen Musik
Telefunken Das Alte Werk SAWT 9532
*PRAETORIUS: 5 CHORALE SETTINGS FOR CHRISTMAS
Ferdinand Conrad Instrumental Ensemble; Niedersachsischer Singkreis, Hannover; Willi Träder, conductor
Nonesuch H-71128

Protestant church music on the Continent has been badly neglected on record. I've yet to encounter anything adequate on the French side. The Germans fare somewhat better, with at least three recordings worthy of note. Ruhland's Stoltzer album includes four psalms in Martin Luther's German translation written between 1524 and 1526 on commission from Queen Mary of Hungary. They are imposingly grand works, monumental in conception, yet marked by the exquisite integration of each tiny detail. Next on my list is still another valuable contribution from the Studio derFrühen Musik (and assisting artists), *Sacred Lieder and Instrumental Music from Luther's Time*. Featured are sacred songs by Senfl, Isaac, Arnold von Bruck, Arnolt Schlick, Cosmas Alder, Lupus Hellinck, and Urbanus Kungsberger. The music is nearly as interesting as the names; Senfl's setting of the Seven Last Words is particularly affecting. Long a special favorite of mine is the Nonesuch album with five of Praetorius's Christmas chorale settings from the *Musae Sionae* (1605-10). These unpretentious settings are moving in their direct simplicity, and the realizations are beyond approach. Also included in this enchanting album are a selection of dances from Praetorius's *Terpsichore* arranged for recorders and percussion and a magnificent pair of stylized dance suites from Schein's *Banchetto Musicale* (1617).

Sacred Polyphony On The Continent

*LASSO: MISSA SUPER "BELL' AMFRIT' ALTERA"; PSALMUS POENITENTIALIS VII
Argo ZRG 735
5 SACRED WORKS
Argo ZRG 795
Choir of Christ Church Cathedral, Oxford, directed by Simon Preston
LASSO: REQUIEM FOR 5 VOICES (1580); O BONE JESU
Harmonia Mundi BASF KHB 20356.
MISSA "PUISQUE J'AY PERDU"; 2 MOTETS
Harmonia Mundi BASF 25 22617-4
Pro Cantione Antiqua of London directed by Bruno Turner
PALESTRINA: MISSA "HODIE CHRISTUS NATUS EST"; 6 MOTETS
Choir of King's College, Cambridge; Philip Ledger, director
EMI ASD 3559 or Angel S-37514

*Palestrina: Missa "Assumpta est Maria"; Antiphon "Assumpta est Maria"; Missa brevis
Argo ZRG 690

Veni sponsa Christi (antiphon, mass, and motet); 5 other sacred works
Argo ZRG 578

Choir of St. John's College, Cambridge; George Guest, director

Palestrina: Missa "Ave Maria"
Choir of King's College Chapel, Cambridge; Philip Ledger, director
EMI HMV ASD 3955. Includes chant Mass Proper

Victoria: Masses and motets on "O quam gloriosum" and "O magnum mysterium"
Soloists, Choir of the Carmelite Priory, London; John McCarthy, conductor
L'Oiseau-Lyre SOL 270

*Victoria: "O quam gloriosum" (mass and motet); other sacred works
Choir of St. John's College, Cambridge; George Guest, director
Argo ZK 70/71 (two discs)

Gesualdo: Responsoria (1611) for Holy Saturday
Escolania de Montserrat conducted by Irene Segarra
DG Archiv 2710 028 (three discs)

*El Siglo De Oro: Spanish Church Music
Pro Cantione Antiqua and The London Cornett & Sackbut Ensemble conducted by Bruno Turner
Telefunken Das Alte Werk 6.35371 (three discs). Concentrates on period 1560–1620

*The Glory of Venice
The Ambrosian Singers with strings and brass conducted by Denis Stevens
Angel S-36443

Sacred Polyphony in England

The Easter Liturgy of the Anglican Church
Oscar Peter, positive organ; London Ambrosian Singers conducted by John McCarthy
Musical Heritage Society MHS 1526/27. Liturgical service featuring music by Byrd, Gibbons, Weelkes, Tallis, Tomkins, Redford, and others

*Byrd/Tallis: Cantiones Sacrae 1575
Cantores in Ecclesia; Michael Howard, director
L'Oiseau-Lyre SOL 311/13 (three discs, available separately)

Byrd: Motets from the Gradualia of 1605 and 1610
William Byrd Choir conducted by Gavin Turner
Philips 9502 030

*Byrd: Masses for 3, 4, and 5 Voices; Sacred Music
Choir of King's College directed by David Willcocks
Argo ZK 53 (two discs)

Byrd: Psalmes, Sonets and Songs of Sadness and Pietie (excerpts)
The Consort of Musicke; Anthony Rooley, director
L'Oiseau-Lyre Florilegium DSLO 596

*Gibbons: Sacred Music
Choir of King's College and Jacobean Consort of Viols directed by David Willcocks. With Simon Preston, organ
Argo ZK 8

TOMKINS: MUSICA DEO SACRA, 1668 (EXCERPTS)
Choir of Magdalen College, Oxford, directed by Bernard Rose
Argo ZRG 897
WEELKES: SACRED MUSIC; ORGAN VOLUNTARY
Choir of St. John's College directed by George Guest
Argo Eclipse ECS 683. With sacred music and organ works by Tallis

For many, the sacred polyphony of the late Renaissance represents the pinnacle of Renaissance achievement. Palestrina, Lasso, Victoria, and Byrd have long been regarded as the greatest figures of this period. To their peerless production of Latin church music should be added, in my opinion, that notable body of Anglican church music of Thomas Tomkins, Thomas Weelkes, and Orlando Gibbons. This music, distinctively British in idiom, possesses every bit as much sublimity as the Latin pieces, and, moreover, has the advantage of being in the English language.

Whether the composer be Italian, Spanish, German, or English, the finest recordings of this late sacred polyphony have been made by British artists. The virtues of these groups should by now be well known. They are nearly all amazingly good—the small groups of men such as the King's Singers and Pro Cantione Antiqua; the larger mixed groups such as the Clerkes of Oxenford and Choir of the Carmelite Priory; and the radiant all-male choruses with boy sopranos such as those of St. John's College, the Westminster Cathedral, and Christ Church Cathedral. The performance styles range from the becoming reserve of Malcolm and Guest to the exciting expressiveness of Howard, McCarthy, and the Pro Cantione. I must single out the last's *El Siglo de Oro,* not because it is musically superior to the others, but because it fills such an important gap in the catalog. This superb anthology audibly demonstrates that while Victoria may represent the culmination of Spanish Renaissance music, the composers who preceded him cannot be ignored. Guerrero in particular emerges as a musician of the first rank.

At the same time these late 16th-century masters were bringing the expressive and sonorous potential of Franco-Flemish polyphony to transcendent heights, Andrea and Giovanni Gabrieli were in Venice exploring the enormous coloristic possibilities of multiple choirs of voices and instruments, each with their own individual parts. The choicest single-disc survey of their music is Denis Stevens's appropriately titled "The Glory of Venice," one of his most impressive efforts. Works such as Giovanni's resplendent motet *In ecclesiis* stretch the language of the Renaissance to its farthest limits. His materials may not be new, but the total effect is so revolutionary that we may safely claim to have crossed the musical border into the Baroque. The end of an incomparable era was at hand.

Further Reading

Blume, Friedrich. *Renaissance and Baroque Music*. New York: Norton, 1967. Includes a brilliant and terse summary of the Renaissance as it applies to music.

Brown, Howard. *Music in the Renaissance*. Englewood Cliffs: Prentice-Hall, 1976. Most recent important study; richly informative.

Brown, Howard. "Performing Practice" in *The New Grove* (qv). Best concise summary of recent research and thought on performance practice.

Dart, Thurston. *The Interpretation of Music*. New York: Harper & Row, 1954. Lively, witty, provocative, and exceedingly thoughtful introduction to fascinating world of performance practice. Dated by new research; should thus be supplemented by Brown's article listed above.

Early Music. Oxford University Press. Elegant British quarterly; best way to keep up with the latest theories and discoveries concerning performance practice and with new recordings of medieval and Renaissance music.

Grout, Donald. *A History of Western Music*. New York: Norton, 1960. Classic single-volume history of Western music; extremely well-written and admirably balanced.

The New Grove Dictionary of Music and Musicians, edited by Stanley Sadie/Macmillan; 1980 (20 vol.) Most important musical reference book to appear in the English language in 25 years. The indispensable source for up-to-date, expert information and comprehensive bibliographies on practically any musical subject.

Harvard Dictionary of Music. Cambridge: Harvard University Press, 1978. Best single-volume musical dictionary. Available in Brief, Concise, or full size.

Hoppin, Richard. *Medieval Music*. New York: Norton, 1978. Most recent important study; extremely detailed.

Reese, Gustave. *Music in the Middle Ages*. New York: Norton, 1940.

——*Music in the Renaissance*. New York: Norton, revised edition, 1959. The standard studies; incredibly thorough and reliable, but more in the nature of encyclopedic references than books to be read through. The medieval book in particular is now severely out-of-date.

Seay, Albert. *Music in the Medieval World*. Englewood Cliffs: Prentice-Hall; be sure to get the 1975 revised edition. Finest succinct survey.

Winn, James. *Unsuspected Eloquence: A History of the Relations between Poetry and Music*. New Haven: Yale University Press, 1981. A most stimulating study, full of provocative ideas.

Obtaining Records

While there is no want of recordings of medieval and Renaissance music, these records are not always readily found in stores; in some instances their very existence can require Holmesian skill and patience to uncover. The standard guides to availability are: in the US, the monthly *The Schwann-1 Record and Tape Guide* (Schwann Record Catalogs; 535 Boylston Street, Boston, MA 02116), and in the UK, the quarterly *Gramophone Classical Catalogue* (177–179 Kenton Road; Harrow, Middlesex, HA3 OHA). No one seriously interested in early music should overlook the vast catalog of the Musical Heritage Society (address below), most of whose records can be obtained only through the mails and are consequently not listed in either the Schwann or Gramophone catalogs. Another flaw of the Schwann is its failure to list the individual pieces in most recorded anthologies. Those readers seeking detailed information of this sort are directed to the two discographies discussed in my Introduction: Coover and Colvig's *Medieval and Renaissance Music on Long-Playing Records,* and Trevor Croucher's *Early Music Discography.* A problem with such undertakings is that they are rarely revised often enough to remain current.

The best way to keep track of new recordings of early music is through the pages of the monthly *Gramophone* (same address as for their catalog) and quarterly *Early Music* (Journals Manager, Oxford University Press; Press Road; Neasden, London MW10 ODD) in Great Britain and the bimonthly *Fanfare* (P.O. Box 720; Tenafly, NJ 07670) in the US. These publications also review records—those in the two British periodicals are particularly well informed. Also useful are the reviews in *High Fidelity* (P.O. Box 10759; Des Moines, Iowa 50430; USA), though that periodical's space allotment to medieval and Renaissance music is not extensive.

Those unfortunate enough to live in an area without access to a major record shop will probably have to resort to mail order to obtain records from some of the smaller labels discussed herein. Each issue of *Gramophone* lists many British firms specializing in exports. Five major US importers of recordings of early music (addresses below) are: Qualiton, Harmonia Mundi U.S.A., International Book and Record Distributors (IBR), German News Company, and Audio Source. All may be ordered from directly. Qualiton specializes in Eastern European labels, Harmonia Mundi U.S.A. in French. German News, as their name suggests, is particularly strong on German labels, such as EMI Reflexe; IBR also imports the Reflexe series, and in addition has a wide selection of titles from EMI of England, France, Italy, and Sweden, as well as from the French Erato label. Audio Source is the US distributor of Hyperion and Astreé. An excellent survey of major US mail-order firms, with detailed commentary on most of those listed below, may be found in the September 1982 issue of the American audiophile publication *The Absolute Sound* (Box L; Sea Cliff, NY 11579).

If a record has gone out-of-print, by far the largest source for cut-outs (all unplayed) is the Berkshire Record Outlet, whose catalogs contain endless bargains of every description—heaven or hell, depending on your budget. Another good cut-out source is Rose Records, who like Berkshire issue periodic catalogs of such items. Both outfits deal in new recordings as well. The used recording market is of course extremely volatile. But if you want a record badly enough, you can probably get it—for a price. Scour the ads in the record magazines for dealers.

With a little effort and the aid of the resources mentioned above and listed below, you should be able to locate a copy of all but the most obscure albums. Almost all the mail-order firms will supply catalogues of their holdings—some are free, some aren't.

MAIL ORDER OUTLETS

UNITED STATES

Allegro Imports
2317 N.E. 15th Avenue
Portland, Oregon 97212

Audio Source
1185 Chess Drive
Foster City, California 94404

Berkshire Record Outlet
428 Pittsfield-Lenox Road
Lenox, Mssachusetts 01240

The Discophile, Inc.
26 West 8th Street
New York, NY 10036

German News
218 East 86th Street
New York, NY 10028

Harmonia Mundi U.S.A.
2351 Westwood Boulevard
Los Angeles, California 90064

International Book and Record Distributors
40-11 24th Street
Long Island City, New York 11101

Musical Heritage Society
14 Park Road
Tinton Falls, New Jersey 07724

Andre Perrault
The Old Stone House
73 East Allen Street
Winooski, Vermont 05404

Qualiton Imports, Ltd.
39028 Crescent Street
Long Island City, New York 11101

Records International
Box 1140
Goleta, California 93116

Rose Records
214 South Wabash Avenue
Chicago, Illinois 60604

Serenade Record Shop, Inc.
Mail Order Department
1713 G Street N.W.
Washington, D.C. 20006

GREAT BRITAIN

Farringdons
28 Holborn Viaduct
London EC1

Harold Moores Records
2 Great Marlborough Street
London, W1

The Music Discount Center, Ltd.
Mail Order Department
47–51 Chalton Street
London NW1 1HY

Tandy's Records Ltd.
24 Islington Row
Birmingham B15 1LJ

Templar Record Shops Ltd.
9a Irving Street
London WC2

Michael G. Thomas
54 Lymington Road
London NW6 1JB

INDEX